THE UNIVERS

The Rights of Others

The Rights of Others examines the boundaries of political
community by focusing on political membership – the principles
and practices for incorporating aliens and strangers, immigrants
and newcomers, refugees and asylum seekers, into existing polities.
Boundaries define some as members, others as aliens. But when
state sovereignty is becoming frayed, and national citizenship is
unraveling, definitions of political membership become much less
clear. Indeed, few issues in world politics today are more important,
or more troubling. In her Seeley Lectures, the distinguished
political theorist Seyla Benhabib makes a powerful plea, echoing
Immanuel Kant, for moral universalism and cosmopolitan
federalism. She advocates not open but porous boundaries,
recognizing not only the admittance rights of refugees and asylum
seekers, but also the regulatory rights of democracies. *The Rights of
Others* is a major intervention in contemporary political theory, of
interest to large numbers of students and specialists in politics, law,
philosophy, and international relations.

SEYLA BENHABIB is one of the leading political theorists in the
world today and Eugene Meyer Professor of Political Science and
Philosophy at Yale University.

The John Robert Seeley Lectures have been established by the University of Cambridge as a biennial lecture series in social and political studies, sponsored jointly by the Faculty of History and Cambridge University Press. The Seeley Lectures provide a unique forum for distinguished scholars of international reputation to address, in an accessible manner, themes of broad and topical interest in social and political studies. Subsequent to their public delivery in Cambridge the University Press publishes suitably modified versions of each sets of lectures. Professor James Tully delivered the inaugural series of Seeley Lectures in 1994 on the theme of *Constitutionalism in an Age of Diversity*.

The Seeley Lectures include

THE RIGHTS OF OTHERS

Aliens, Residents, and Citizens

SEYLA BENHABIB
Yale University

CAMBRIDGE
UNIVERSITY PRESS

CAMBRIDGE
UNIVERSITY PRESS

University Printing House, Cambridge CB2 8BS, United Kingdom

Cambridge University Press is part of the University of Cambridge.

It furthers the University's mission by disseminating knowledge in the pursuit of education, learning and research at the highest international levels of excellence.

www.cambridge.org
Information on this title: www.cambridge.org/9780521538602

© Seyla Benhabib 2004

First published 2004
9th printing 2011

A catalogue record for this publication is available from the British Library

Library of Congress Cataloguing in Publication data
Benhabib, Seyla.
The rights of others: aliens, residents, and citizens
   p.   cm. – (The John Robert Seeley Lectures ; 5)
Includes bibliographical references and index.
ISBN 0 521 83134 2 – ISBN 0 521 53860 2 (pbk.)
1. Political rights.   2. Internationalism.   3. Citizenship.   4. Emigration and immigration.   5. Aliens – Civil rights.   6. Refugees – Civil rights.   7. Immigrants – Civil rights.   I. Title.   II. Series.
JF799.B44   2004
323.3'291 – dc22   2004045665

ISBN 978-0-521-83134-5 Hardback
ISBN 978-0-521-53860-2 Paperback

"No human is illegal"

Immigrant Workers' Freedom Ride 2003

October 4, 2003

Queens, New York

CONTENTS

ACKNOWLEDGMENTS

This book presents the revised and expanded version of the John Robert Seeley Lectures, delivered at the invitation of the University of Cambridge in King's College on April 27–May 2, 2002. I thank Gareth Stedman Jones and Miri Rubin for their generous hospitality during this period. Special thanks go to Quentin Skinner under whose auspices I was first invited to deliver them. Susan James, Istvan Hont, Onora O'Neill, John Dunn, Richard Tuck, Emma Rothschild, Amartya Sen, and Andrew Kuper enriched my stay in Cambridge through their questions and comments.

Among the many occasions on which I presented the ideas gathered in this volume, the discussion at the Yale Law School's Legal Theory Colloquium in February 2002 was one of the most memorable. My thanks to Dean Anthony Kronman, who presided, and to my colleagues Bruce Ackerman, Owen Fiss, Paul Kahn, Judith Resnik, and Reva Siegel for subsequent conversations and remarks. I am particularly grateful to Judith Resnik for supplying me with pertinent international law references.

My colleagues at the University of Toronto, Joseph Carens, Melissa Williams, Audrey Macklin, and Jennifer Nedelsky, heard me present some of this material under the auspices of the Priestley lectureship in October 2003. I am grateful to them for their incisive comments.

For their questions and reflections on Kant, Arendt, and the European Union, I also thank Veit Bader, Rainer Bauboeck, Jay Bernstein, Richard J. Bernstein, James Bohman, Nancy Fraser, Morris Kaplan, Riva Kastoryano, John McCormick, Max Pensky, Ulrich Preuss, and Sayres Rudy. I am particularly grateful to Carolin Emcke for her thoughts on chapters 3 and 5, and to Nancy Kokaz for her spirited defense of Rawls against my criticisms. Special thanks go to Willem Maas for many conversations on citizenship within the European Union, and in particular for his help with chapter 4. Melvin Rogers was an indispensable assistant in preparing the bibliography and helping me with references throughout. David Leslie provided crucial copyediting assistance in the final stages of this book.

A special word of gratitude is due to my family, my daughter, Laura and my husband, Jim Sleeper, who have accompanied me from Boston to Amsterdam, to London, to Istanbul, and to Connecticut, as this book took shape over many voyages, border crossings, and passport controls.

Parts of chapter 1 have previously appeared as "Of Guests, Aliens and Citizens: Rereading Kant's Cosmopolitan Right," in *Pluralism and the Pragmatic Turn: The Transformation of Critical Theory. Essays in Honor of Thomas McCarthy* ed. by William Rehg and James Bohman (Cambridge, MA: MIT Press, 2001). Chapter 2 has been published in part as "Political Geographies in a Changing World: Arendtian Reflections," *Social Research*, 69 (2) (Summer 2002): 539–556; material from chapter 4 is included in "Transformations of Citizenship: The Case of Contemporary Europe," *Government and Opposition*,

37 (4) (Fall 2002): 439–465. My Seeley Lectures expand, revise, and continue reflections which I initiated in my Spinoza Lectures under the title *Transformations of Citizenship: Dilemmas of the Nation-State in the Era of Globalization* (Amsterdam: Van Gorcum, 2001), copyright Seyla Benhabib.

Finally, many thanks to Richard Fisher, Karen Anderson Howes, and Alison Powell of Cambridge University Press. It was a pleasure to work with them.

PREFACE

At the dawn of a new century the trans-national movement of peoples has emerged as a major issue of our times. Whether they are initiated by economic migrants from the poorer regions of the world trying to reach the shores of resource-rich democracies in the north and the west; whether they are undertaken by asylum and refuge seekers escaping persecution, civil wars, and natural disasters; or whether they are initiated by 'displaced persons,' who are fleeing civil war, ethnic conflict and state-inflicted violence in their own societies, such movements have presented the world-state system with unprecedented challenges. Given the salience of these developments, it is surprising that the cross-border movements of peoples, and the philosophical as well as policy problems suggested by them, have been the object of such scant attention in contemporary political philosophy. *The Rights of Others* intended to fill this lacuna in contemporary political thought by focusing on *political membership.*

I am grateful that my arguments have aroused a good deal of attention. *The Rights of Others* has won the Ralph Bunche Award of the American Political Science Association in 2005, and was given the Best Book in Social Philosophy award in 2004 by the North American Society for Social Philosophy. Also, the book has been translated into Spanish, Italian, Turkish, Dutch, and Chinese, with a German translation forthcoming.

Two symposia enabled me to engage with my critics: the proceedings of the symposium held by the North American Society for Social Philosophy appears in *Science, Technology, and Social Justice*, edited by John Rowan (Social Philosophy Today Book Series, vol. 22, Philosophy Documentation Center, 2007); *The European Journal of Political Theory* in its volume 6, No. 4 (Fall 2007) contains a special section devoted to *The Rights of Others*.

Finally, since I completed writing on the "scarf affair" in France and on the rights of third-country nationals within the European Union in winter of 2004 (chapters 4 and 5), there have been further political developments in both areas but they do not affect the gist of the analysis presented here. If anything, the issue of Islam in Europe, and in particular the rights of Muslim women, have become even more salient than at the time I completed this book; and after the defeat of the European Constitution in the summer of 2005, the subject of the harmonization of the rights of third-country nationals across the EU is still on the agenda.

June 2007
Berkshires, Massachusetts

This book examines the boundaries of political community by focusing on political membership. By *political membership*, I mean the principles and practices for incorporating aliens and strangers, immigrants and newcomers, refugees and asylum seekers, into existing polities. Political boundaries define some as members, others as aliens. Membership, in turn, is meaningful only when accompanied by rituals of entry, access, belonging, and privilege. The modern nation-state system has regulated membership in terms of one principal category: national citizenship. We have entered an era when state sovereignty has been frayed, and the institution of national citizenship has been disaggregated or unbundled into diverse elements. New modalities of membership have emerged, with the result that the boundaries of the political community, as defined by the nation-state system, are no longer adequate to regulate membership.

Political membership has rarely been considered an important aspect of domestic or international justice. Along with the "invisibility" of state boundaries, the practices and institutions regulating access to and exit from political membership have also been invisible and not subject to theoretical scrutiny and analysis. I want to argue that transnational migrations, and the constitutional as well as policy issues suggested by the movement of peoples across state borders, are central

1

to interstate relations and therefore to a normative theory of global justice.

Recent attempts to develop theories of international and global justice have been curiously silent on the matter of migration (see Pogge 1992; Buchanan 2000; Beitz [1979] 1999 and 2000). Despite their criticism of state-centric assumptions, these theorists have not questioned the fundamental cornerstone of state centrism, which is the policing and protecting of state boundaries against foreigners and intruders, refugees and asylum seekers. The control of migration – of immigration as well as emigration – is crucial to state sovereignty. All pleas to develop "post-Westphalian" conceptions of sovereignty (Buchanan 2000 and 2001) are ineffective if they do not also address the normative regulation of peoples' movement across territorial boundaries. From a philosophical point of view, transnational migrations bring to the fore the constitutive dilemma at the heart of liberal democracies: between sovereign self-determination claims on the one hand and adherence to universal human rights principles on the other. I will argue that practices of political membership are best illuminated through an *internal reconstruction* of these dual commitments.

There is not only a tension, but often an outright contradiction, between human rights declarations and states' sovereign claims to control their borders as well as to monitor the quality and quantity of admittees. There are no easy solutions to the dilemmas posed by these dual commitments. I will not call for the end of the state system nor for world citizenship. Rather, following the Kantian tradition of cosmopolitan federalism, I will underscore the significance of membership within bounded communities and defend the need for "democratic attachments" that may not be directed toward existing nation-state structures alone. Quite to the contrary: as the institution of citizenship is disaggregated (see ch. 4) and state sovereignty comes under increasing stress, subnational as well as supra-national spaces for democratic attachments and agency are emerging in the contemporary world, and they ought to be advanced with, rather than in lieu of, existing polities. It is important to respect the claims of diverse democratic communities, including their distinctive cultural, legal, and constitutional self-understandings, while strengthening their commitments to emerging norms of cosmopolitical justice.

My position differs from recent neo-Kantian theories of international justice which give precedence to matters of distribution of resources and rights over questions of membership. I argue that a cosmopolitan theory of justice cannot be restricted to schemes of *just distribution* on a global scale, but must also incorporate a vision of *just membership*. Such just membership entails: recognizing the moral claim of refugees and asylees to *first admittance*; a regime of *porous* borders for immigrants; an injunction against denationalization and the loss of citizenship rights; and the vindication of the right of every human being "to have rights," that is, to be a *legal person*, entitled to certain inalienable rights, regardless of the status of their political membership. The status of alienage ought not to denude one of fundamental rights. Furthermore, just membership also entails the right to citizenship on the part of the alien who has fulfilled certain conditions. Permanent alienage is not only incompatible with a liberal-democratic understanding of human community; it is also a violation of fundamental human

rights. The right to political membership must be accommo-
dated by practices that are non-discriminatory in scope, transparent in formulation and execution, and justiciable when
violated by states and other state-like organs. The doctrine
of state sovereignty, which has so far shielded naturalization, citizenship, and denationalization decisions from scrutiny
by international as well as constitutional courts, must be
challenged.

Crisis of territoriality

Questions of political boundaries and membership
have become particularly salient because the Westphalian
model of state sovereignty is in crisis for many reasons.[1] The
"Westphalian model" presupposes that there is a dominant and
unified political authority whose jurisdiction over a clearly
marked piece of territory is supreme. This model's efficacy
and normative relevance are being challenged by the rise of
a global economy through the formation of free markets in
capital, finance, and labor; the increasing internationalization of armament, communication, and information tech-
nologies; the emergence of international and transnational
cultural networks and electronic spheres; and the growth of
sub- and transnational political actors. Globalization draws
the administrative-material functions of the state into increasingly volatile contexts that far exceed any one state's capacities
to influence decisions and outcomes. The nation-state is too
small to deal with the economic, ecological, immunological,

---

[1] Stephen Krasner (1999) has expressed skepticism about the historical
dominance of this model, but I believe that its normative force in
ordering interstate relations is not equally in question.

and informational problems created by the new environment; yet it is too large to accommodate the aspirations of identity-driven social and regionalist movements. Under these conditions, *territoriality* has become an anachronistic delimitation of material functions and cultural identities; yet, even in the face of the collapse of traditional concepts of sovereignty, monopoly over territory is exercised through immigration and citizenship policies.

It is estimated that, whereas in 1910 roughly 33 million individuals lived in countries other than their own as migrants, by the year 2000 that number had reached 175 million. During this same period (1910–2000), the population of the world is estimated to have grown from 1.6 to 5.3 billion, that is threefold (Zlotnik 2001, 227). Migrations, by contrast, increased almost sixfold over the course of these ninety years. Strikingly, more than half of the increase of migrants from 1910 to 2000 occurred in the last three and a half decades of the twentieth century, between 1965 and 2000. In this period 75 million people undertook crossborder movements to settle in countries other than that of their origin (United Nations, Department of Economic and Social Affairs 2002).

While migratory movements in the latter half of the twentieth century have accelerated, the plight of refugees has also grown. There are almost 20 million refugees, asylum seekers, and "internally displaced persons" in the world. The resource-rich countries of Europe and the northern hemisphere face a growing number of migrants, but it is mostly nations in the southern hemisphere, such as Chad, Pakistan, and Ingushetia, that are home to hundreds of thousands of refugees fleeing wars in the neighboring countries of the

5

Central African Republic, Afghanistan, and Chechnya (Rieff 2003).

As one thoughtful student of worldwide immigration trends has observed, "Over the past one hundred years, international migration has often been at the center stage of major events that reshaped the world. The twentieth century began with a decade in which transatlantic migration reached unprecedented levels and it has closed with one in which migration from developing to developed countries and from Eastern bloc countries to the West has been at a high" (Zlotnik 2001, 257).

To acknowledge such trends need not commit one to exaggerated claims about the "end" of the state system. The irony of current political developments is that, while state sovereignty in economic, military, and technological domains has been greatly eroded, it is nonetheless vigorously asserted, and national borders, while more porous, are still there to keep out aliens and intruders. The old political structures may have waned but the new political forms of globalization are not yet in sight.

We are like travelers navigating an unknown terrain with the help of old maps, drawn at a different time and in response to different needs. While the terrain we are traveling on, the world society of states, has changed, our normative map has not. I do not pretend to have a new map to replace the old one, but I do hope to contribute to a better understanding of the salient fault-lines of the unknown territory which we are traversing. The growing normative incongruities between international human rights norms, particularly as they pertain to the "rights of others" – immigrants, refugees, and asylum seekers – and assertions of territorial sovereignty are the novel features of this new landscape.

An international human rights regime

The period since the Universal Declaration of Human Rights of 1948 has witnessed the emergence of international human rights norms. Crossborder movements of peoples, and particularly those of refugees and asylees, are now subject to an international human rights regime.[2] By an international human rights regime, I understand a set of interrelated and overlapping global and regional regimes that encompass human rights treaties as well as customary international law or international "soft law" (an expression used to describe international agreements which are not treaties and therefore are not covered by the Vienna Convention on the Law of Treaties) (Neuman, 2003).

[2] Examples would include the UN treaty bodies under the International Covenant on Civil and Political Rights, the International Covenant on Economic, Social and Cultural Rights, the Convention on the Elimination of All Forms of Racial Discrimination, the Convention on the Elimination of All Forms of Discrimination Against Women, the Convention Against Torture and Other Cruel, Inhuman or Degrading Treatment or Punishment, and the Convention on the Rights of the Child (Neuman 2003). The establishment of the European Union has been accompanied by a Charter of Fundamental Rights and by the formation of a European Court of Justice. The European Convention for the Protection of Human Rights and Fundamental Freedoms, which encompasses states that are not EU members as well, permits the claims of citizens of adhering states to be heard by a European Court of Human Rights. Parallel developments can be seen on the American continent through the establishment of the Inter-American System for the Protection of Human Rights and the Inter-American Court of Human Rights (Jacobson 1997, 75).

We are witnessing this development in at least three interrelated areas.

Crimes against humanity, genocide, and war crimes

The concept of *crimes against humanity*, first articulated by the Allied powers in the Nuremberg trials of Nazi war criminals, stipulates that there are certain norms in accordance with which state officials as well as private individuals are to treat one another, even, and precisely, under conditions of extreme hostility and war. Ethnic cleansing, mass executions, rape, and cruel and unusual punishment of the enemy, such as dismemberment, which occur under conditions of a "widespread or systematic attack," are proscribed, and all can constitute sufficient grounds for the indictment and prosecution of individuals who are responsible for these actions, even if they are or were state officials, or subordinates who acted under orders. The refrain of the soldier and the bureaucrat – "I was only doing my duty" – is no longer an acceptable ground for abrogating the rights of humanity in the person of the other – even when, and especially when, the other is your enemy.

The continuing rearticulation of these categories in international law, and in particular their extension from situations of international armed conflict to civil wars within a country and to the actions of governments against their own people, has in turn encouraged the emergence of the concept of "humanitarian interventions."[3]

---

[3] During the Nuremberg trials, "crimes against humanity" was used to refer to crimes committed during international armed conflicts. (United Nations 1945, Art. 6 [c]; see Ratner and Abrams [1997] 2002, 26–45;

Humanitarian interventions

The theory and practice of humanitarian interventions, which the USA and its NATO allies appealed to in order to justify their actions against ethnic cleansing and continuing crimes against the civilian population in Bosnia and Kosovo, suggest that, when a sovereign nation-state egregiously violates the basic human rights of a segment of its population

Schabas 2001, 6–7). Immediately after the Nuremberg trials, genocide was also included as a crime against humanity but was left distinct, due its own jurisdictional status which was codified in Article II of the Convention on the Prevention and Punishment of the Crime of Genocide (1948). *Genocide* is the knowing and willful destruction of the way of life and existence of a collectivity whether through acts of total war, racial extinction, or ethnic cleansing. It is the supreme crime against humanity, in that it aims at the destruction of human variety, of the many and diverse ways of being human. Genocide not only eliminates individuals who may belong to this or another group; it aims at the extinction of their way of life – the intent requirement (Ratner and Abrams [1997] 2002, 35–36).

    War crimes, by contrast, as defined in the Statute of the International Criminal Tribunal for the Former Yugoslavia (United Nations 1993), initially only applied to *international conflicts*. With the Statute of the International Criminal Tribunal for Rwanda (United Nations 1994), recognition was extended to *internal armed conflict* as well. "War crimes" now refer to international as well as internal conflicts that involve the mistreatment or abuse of civilians and non-combatants as well as one's enemy in combat (Ratner and Abrams [1997] 2002, 80–110; Schabas 2001, 40–53). Thus, in a significant development since World War II, crimes against humanity, genocide, and war crimes have all been extended to apply not only to atrocities that take place in international conflict situations, but also to events *within* the borders of a sovereign country and that may be perpetrated by officials of that country and/or by its citizens during peacetime. I wish to thank Melvin Rogers for his special assistance in clarifying these concepts and developments in international law.

on account of their religion, race, ethnicity, language, and culture, there is a *generalized moral obligation* to end actions such as genocide and crimes against humanity (Buchanan 2001). In such cases human rights norms trump state sovereignty claims. No matter how controversial in interpretation and application they may be, humanitarian interventions are based on the growing consensus that the sovereignty of the state to dispose over the life, liberty, and property of its citizens or residents is neither unconditional nor unlimited (Doyle 2001). State sovereignty is no longer the ultimate arbiter of the fate of citizens or residents. The exercise of state sovereignty even within domestic borders is increasingly subject to internationally recognized norms which prohibit genocide, ethnocide, mass expulsions, enslavement, rape, and forced labor.

Transnational migration

The third area in which international human rights norms are creating binding guidelines upon the will of sovereign nation-states is that of international migration. *Humanitarian interventions* deal with the treatment by nation-states of their citizens or residents; *crimes against humanity* and *war crimes* concern relations among enemies or opponents in nationally bounded as well as extra-territorial settings. *Transnational migrations*, by contrast, pertain to the rights of individuals, not insofar as they are considered members of concrete bounded communities but insofar as they are human beings *simpliciter*, when they come into contact with, seek entry into, or want to become members of territorially bounded communities.

The Universal Declaration of Human Rights (United Nations 1948) recognizes the right to freedom of movement across boundaries: a right to emigrate – that is, to leave a country – but not a right to immigrate – a right to enter a country (Article 13). Article 14 anchors the right to enjoy asylum under certain circumstances, while Article 15 of the Declaration proclaims that everyone has "the right to a nationality." The second half of Article 15 stipulates that "No one shall be arbitrarily deprived of his nationality nor denied the right to change his nationality" (www.unhchr.ch/udhr/lang/eng.htm).

The Universal Declaration is silent on states' *obligations* to grant entry to immigrants, to uphold the right of asylum, and to permit citizenship to alien residents and denizens. These rights have no specific addressees and they do not appear to anchor *specific* obligations on the part of second and third parties to comply with them. Despite the crossborder character of these rights, the Declaration upholds the sovereignty of individual states. Thus a series of internal contradictions between universal human rights and territorial sovereignty are built into the logic of the most comprehensive international law documents in our world.

The Geneva Convention of 1951 Relating to the Status of Refugees and its Protocol added in 1967 are the second most important international legal documents governing crossborder movements. Nevertheless, neither the existence of these documents nor the creation of the United Nations High Commissioner on Refugees have altered the fact that this Convention and its Protocol are binding on signatory states alone and can be brazenly disregarded by non-signatories and, at times, even by signatory states themselves.

Some lament the fact that, as international human rights norms are increasingly invoked in immigration, refugee, and asylum disputes, territorially delimited nations are challenged not only in their claims to control their borders but also in their prerogative to define the "boundaries of the national community" (Jacobson 1997, 5). Others criticize the Universal Declaration for not endorsing "institutional cosmopolitanism," and for upholding an "interstatal" rather than a truly cosmopolitan international order (O'Neill 2000, 180). Yet one thing is clear: the treatment by states of citizens and residents within their boundaries is no longer an unchecked prerogative. One of the cornerstones of Westphalian sovereignty, namely that states enjoy ultimate authority over all objects and subjects within their circumscribed territory, has been delegitimized through international law.

What then should be guiding normative principles of membership in a world of increasingly deterritorialized politics? Which practices and principles of civil and political incorporation are most compatible with the philosophical self-understanding and constitutional commitments of liberal democracies? These are the principal questions that I address by exploring the philosophical as well as institutional aspects of political membership in liberal democracies.

Discourse theory and political membership

I approach political membership from the standpoint of discourse ethics and a normative theory of deliberative democracy (see Benhabib 1992; [1996] 2003; 2002a). Membership and attendant questions of inclusion and exclusion have been vexing for discourse theory since its inception. The basic premise of discourse ethics states that "only those norms and normative institutional arrangements are valid which can be agreed to by all concerned under special argumentation situations named discourses" (see Habermas [1983] 1990; Benhabib 1992, 29–67; 2002a, 107–114). I call this principle a *metanorm*, in that more specific norms that can be deemed valid need to be tested through procedures that can meet this criterion. In my interpretation, this metanorm presupposes the principles of *universal moral respect* and *egalitarian reciprocity*. *Universal respect* means that we recognize the rights of all beings capable of speech and action to be participants in the moral conversation; the principle of *egalitarian reciprocity*, interpreted within the confines of discourse ethics, stipulates that in discourses each should have the same rights to various speech acts, to initiate new topics, and to ask for justification of the presuppositions of the conversations.

Within discourse ethics, the problem of *scope*, the question of who ought to be included or not in discourses, has always posed a difficulty. On first reading the theory seems to exclude from moral agency and moral representation those who are not capable of full speech and action. Depending on how strongly "the capacity for speech and action" is defined, many beings whom we would want to recognize as moral agents and as moral victims, such as very young children, the differently abled, and the mentally ill, would seem to be excluded from the moral conversation. Furthermore, there may be beings to whom we *owe* moral obligations and who may become moral victims by virtue of being impacted by our actions but who cannot represent themselves: sentient beings capable of pain,

13

such as animals with developed nervous systems and, some would argue, even trees and ecosystems, are alive and can be affected by our actions. Can discourse ethics do justice to their moral claims and to their moral plight? I have suggested in other contexts that the moral interests of beings who are not full participants in moral discourses ought to be and can be effectively represented in discursive contexts through systems of moral advocacy (Benhabib 1992, 58 n. 30; 2002a, 190–191, n. 7).

Considered with respect to political membership claims, the problem of *discursive scope* poses a different set of difficulties. Since discourse theory articulates a universalist moral standpoint, it cannot limit the scope of the *moral conversation* only to those who reside within nationally recognized boundaries; it must view the moral conversation as potentially extending to all of *humanity*. Put starkly, every person, and every moral agent who has interests and whom my actions and the consequences of my actions can impact and affect in some manner or another, is potentially a moral-conversation partner with me: I have a moral obligation to *justify my actions with reasons* to this individual or to the representatives of this being. I respect the moral worth of the other by recognizing that I must provide them with a justification for my actions. We are all potential participants in such conversations of justification. The stipulations of discourse ethics, therefore, cannot be extended into the domain of political membership without the aid of further normative elaboration, nor is it necessary to do so. A discursive approach should place *significant limitations* on what can count as *morally permissible* practices of inclusion and exclusion within sovereign polities.

Due to the open-endedness of discourses of moral justification there will be an inevitable and necessary tension between moral obligations and duties resulting from our membership in bounded communities and the moral perspective which we must adopt as human beings *simpliciter*. From a universalist and cosmopolitan point of view, boundaries, including state borders and frontiers, require justification. Practices of inclusion and exclusion are always subject to questioning from the standpoint of the infinitely open moral conversation.

This confronts the discourse theorist who is examining political-membership practices with a dilemma: a shared feature of all norms of membership, including but not only norms of citizenship, is that those who are affected by the consequences of these norms and, in the first place, by criteria of exclusion, *per definitionem*, cannot be party to their articulation. Membership norms affect those who are not members precisely by distinguishing insiders from outsiders, citizens from non-citizens. The dilemma is this: either a discourse theory is simply *irrelevant* to membership practices in that it cannot articulate *any* justifiable criteria of exclusion, or it simply *accepts* existing practices of exclusion as *morally neutral* historical contingencies that require no further validation. But this would suggest that a discourse theory of democracy is itself chimerical insofar as democracy would seem to require a morally justifiable closure which discourse ethics cannot deliver.

Unlike communitarians who reduce the demands of morality to the claims of specific ethical, cultural, and political communities, and unlike realists and postmodernists who are skeptical that political norms can ever be made subordinate to moral ones, the discourse ethicist insists upon *the necessary disjunction as well as the necessary mediation between the moral and the ethical, the moral and the political.* The task for her is one of mediations, not reductions. How can one mediate moral universalism with ethical particularism? How can one mediate legal and political norms with moral ones? Questions of membership confront us continuously with such challenges of mediation: if we do not differentiate between *the moral and the ethical,* we cannot criticize the exclusionary citizenship and membership practices of specific cultural, religious, and ethnic communities. And if we do not differentiate between *morality and legality,* we cannot criticize the legally enacted norms of democratic majorities even if they refuse to admit refugees to their midst, turn away asylum seekers at the door, and shut off their borders to immigrants. Finally, if we do not differentiate between *morality and functionality,* we cannot challenge practices of immigration, naturalization, and border control for violating our cherished moral, constitutional, and ethical beliefs.

Our fate, as late-modern individuals, is to live caught in the permanent tug of war between the vision of the universal and the attachments of the particular. In a "disenchanted universe," in Weber's sense, competing values clamor for our allegiance (Weber [1922] 1958, 147–156). Although for Weber this condition meant an unavoidable and inevitable polytheism of values, for me it suggests the bad faith of all attempts which try to simplify the field of moral tension by eliminating important aspects of our multiple and conflicting allegiances. Just as we cannot cease to mediate the needs of our loved ones with the demands of impersonal, institutional obligations; just as we cannot cease to measure the actions of our polities in light of the claims of strangers; just as we cannot cease to participate in dialogues with those who worship different gods than ourselves, so too we cannot collapse the moral universal into the particular, the legal, or the functional.

Can there be a discourse-theoretical justification of democratic closure, then? This book answers that there are some practices of democratic closure which are more justifiable than others but that potentially all practices of democratic closure are open to challenge, resignification, and deinstitutionalization. The project of postnational solidarity is a moral project that transcends existing state boundaries, and nowhere are the tensions between the demands of postnational universalistic solidarity and the practices of exclusive membership more apparent than at the site of territorial borders and boundaries.

In "The European Nation-State," Jürgen Habermas has observed:

> There is a conceptual gap in the legal construction of the constitutional state, a gap that is tempting to fill with a naturalistic conception of the people. One cannot explain in purely normative terms how the universe of those who come together to regulate their common life by means of positive law should be composed. From a normative point of view, the social boundaries of an association of free and equal associates under law are perfectly contingent. (1998, 115–116)

Since the nineteenth century, and extending to the state formations that emerged after decolonization and the end of communism, this "conceptual gap" has been filled by the ideology and practice of nationalism. Citizenship and practices of political membership are the rituals through which the nation is reproduced spatially. The control of territorial boundaries, which is coeval with the sovereignty of the modern nation-state, seeks to ensure the purity of the nation *in time* through the policing of its contacts and interactions *in space*. The history of citizenship reveals that these nationalist aspirations are ideologies; they attempt to mold a complex, unruly, and unwieldy reality according to some simple governing principle of reduction, such as national membership. Every nation has its others, within and without (see Benhabib 2002a). In fact, nationalism is constituted through a series of imaginary as well as very real demarcations between us and them, we and the others. Through membership practices the state controls the synchronic and diachronic identity of the nation. Yet the nationality and citizenship rules of all peoples are an admixture of historical contingencies, territorial struggles, cultural clashes, and bureaucratic fiat. At certain historical junctures, these rules and the struggles surrounding them become more transparent and visible than at other times. We are at such a historical juncture when the problem of political boundaries has once more become visible.

Nationalism offers one solution to the "conceptual gap in the legal construction of the constitutional state." Democratic perspectives, whether liberal, republican, or multicultural offer yet another. But how can we justify the legal construction of the constitutional state? I will follow Habermas in accepting that universal human rights and popular sovereignty, or the norms of private and public autonomy,

18

provide two indispensable foundations of the democratic constitutional state (Habermas 1996, 84–104). Universal human rights have a context-transcending appeal, whereas popular and democratic sovereignty must constitute a circumscribed *demos* which acts to govern itself. Self-governance implies self-constitution. There is thus an irresolvable contradiction, maybe even a "fatal tension" (Cole 2000, 2), between the expansive and inclusionary principles of moral and political universalism, as anchored in universal human rights, and the particularistic and exclusionary conceptions of democratic closure. Carl Schmitt, therefore, argued that liberalism, the belief in universal moral equality, and democracy, the belief in citizens' equality, were necessarily incompatible (Schmitt [1923] 1985). Yet modern constitutional democracies are based upon the faith that these two commitments can be used to limit one another, that they can be renegotiated, rearticulated, and resignified.

I develop the concept of "democratic iterations" to show how commitments to context-transcending constitutional and international norms can be mediated with the will of democratic majorities. Democratic iterations are complex processes of public argument, deliberation, and learning through which universalist right claims are contested and contextualized, invoked and revoked, throughout legal and political institutions as well as in the public sphere of liberal democracies.

Democratic iterations not only change established understandings in a polity but they also transform authoritative precedents. I view democratic iterations as engaging in "jurisgenerative politics" (Cover 1983; Michelman 1988). Through such processes the democratic people shows itself to be not only the *subject* but also the *author of its laws*. The politics of membership, precisely because it bears upon the self-definition and composition of the *demos*, becomes the site of jurisgenerative politics through which the *demos* faces the disjunction between the universalist content of its constitutional commitments and the paradoxes of democratic closure.

Popular sovereignty is not identical with territorial sovereignty, although the two are closely linked, both historically and normatively. Popular sovereignty means that all full members of the *demos* are entitled to have a voice in the articulation of the laws by which the *demos* is to govern itself. Democratic rule, then, extends its jurisdiction in the first place to those who can view themselves as the authors of such rule. As I will argue, however, there has never been a perfect overlap between the circle of those who stand under the law's authority and the full members of the *demos*. Every democratic *demos* has disenfranchised some, while recognizing only certain individuals as full members. Territorial sovereignty and democratic voice have never matched completely. Yet presence within a circumscribed territory, and in particular continuing residence within it, brings one under the authority of the sovereign – whether democratic or not. The new politics of membership is about negotiating this complex relationship between the rights of full membership, democratic voice, and territorial residence.

I argue that such negotiations and democratic iterations take place in the context of a world society of states. Consequently, policies regarding access to citizenship ought not to be viewed as unilateral acts of self-determination, but rather must be seen as decisions with multilateral consequences that influence other entities in the world community. Sovereignty is a relational concept; it is not merely self-referential. Defining the identity of the democratic people is an ongoing process of constitutional self-creation. While the paradox that those who are not members of the *demos* will remain affected by its decisions of inclusion and exclusion can never be completely eliminated, its effects can be mitigated through reflexive acts of democratic iteration by the people who critically examines and alters its own practices of exclusion. We can render the distinctions between "citizens" and "aliens," "us" and "them," fluid and negotiable through democratic iterations. Only then do we move toward a postmetaphysical and postnational conception of cosmopolitan solidarity which increasingly brings all human beings, by virtue of their humanity alone, under the net of universal rights, while chipping away at the exclusionary privileges of membership. The "disaggregation of citizenship rights" in contemporary Europe is the central case study through which these sociological trends toward postnational solidarity are illustrated.

Chapter 1 begins with an examination of Kant's doctrine of cosmopolitan right. I focus on the Third Article of "Perpetual Peace," concerning the right of universal hospitality and the only one in fact which Kant explicitly names "cosmopolitan right" (*Weltbürgerrecht*). I argue that, despite historical concerns which were radically different from ours, Kant set the terms which still guide our thinking on refugee and asylum claims on the one hand, and immigration on the other. Situated between morality and legality, between universal principles of human rights and the established legal orders of individual polities, the right of hospitality demarcates a new

21

level of international law which had been previously restricted to relations among sovereign heads of states.

Chapter 2 considers Hannah Arendt's discussion of "the right to have rights." Reflecting on the predicament of statelessness in Europe during the interwar period of 1918–1939, Arendt provides one of the most penetrating philosophical articulations of the dilemma of rightlessness. Like Kant, she reflects on the inherent conflicts of the state-centric and territorially circumscribed world of international relations from a cosmopolitan standpoint.

While Arendt brilliantly articulates the demise of the Westphalian model of state relations, she can offer no solutions to the dilemmas of the "right to have rights." Partly for institutional, partly for philosophical reasons, she cannot deconstruct the stark dichotomy between human rights and citizens' rights. By contrast, I develop an argument to bridge the gap that she opens up between these two dimensions of rights claims. My strategy is to incorporate citizenship claims into a universal human rights regime.

Chapter 3 outlines the concept of just membership by engaging with contemporary neo-Kantian theories of global justice. I begin with a consideration of John Rawls's *The Law of Peoples*, and analyze why migration is relegated to aspects of non-ideal theory. Contemporary critics of Rawls also neglect migration as a philosophical problem. As a corrective to Rawls's focus on "peoples" (a term whose definition is contested), they articulate cosmopolitan-justice principles for individuals. Global-distributive justice for individuals neglects one of the first principles of distribution, namely the distribution of human beings as members of diverse communities. What are the principles for the just distribution of membership? Contemporary theories of distributive justice not only ignore just membership but also suffer from a "democratic deficit," because they pay little attention to the democratic legitimacy of their *politics* of distribution. There is an implicit tendency in these theories to favor world government or other supra- or transnational political agencies of distribution whose democratic credentials are left in abeyance. Cosmopolitan federalism, by contrast, is a vision of global justice which is also democratic and which proceeds from the interdependence of democracy and distribution. This perspective permits us to reconceptualize transnational migrations.

Chapters 4 and 5 are more institutional and empirical in focus. In chapter 4, I examine the disaggregation of citizenship claims, particularly with reference to the European Union. Collective identity, privileges of political membership, and the entitlement to social benefits are no longer bundled together within a unified institution of national citizenship. They are disaggregated and come under the purview of different rights regimes and multiple, nested sovereignties. Yet disaggregated citizenship is not cosmopolitan citizenship. The developments it describes may be driving the worldwide mobility of peoples without democratic attachments and civic commitments, leading to the formation of a world proletariat, participating in global markets but lacking a *demos*.

Chapter 5 deals with the interpenetration of the local, the global, and the national and highlights the practice of democratic iterations. Cosmopolitan citizenship, I argue, entails the reclaiming and the repositioning of the universal – its iteration – within the framework of the local, the regional, or other sites of democratic activism and engagement. I focus on three cases drawn from recent European developments to illustrate practices of democratic iteration at work: the "scarf affair" in France; the case of a German-Afghani schoolteacher who was denied the right to teach with her head covered and the German Constitutional Court's decision on the matter; and finally a 1990 decision of the German Constitutional Court that denied the right to vote in local elections to long-term foreign residents of the province of Schleswig-Holstein and the city-state of Hamburg. These decisions were superseded in 1993 by the Treaty of Maastricht, but they set in motion a process of democratic iteration which resulted in the abolishing of Germany's rather antiquated and restrictive citizenship laws, dating back to 1913.

1

On hospitality: rereading Kant's cosmopolitan right

This chapter begins with an analysis of Kant's understanding of cosmopolitan right. Kant's discussion focuses on moral and legal relations which hold among individuals *across* bounded communities, and thereby demarcates a novel domain situated between the law of specific polities on the one hand and customary international law on the other. Katrin Flikschuh states this clearly: "Kant recognizes three distinct though related levels of rightful relation: the 'Right of a State' specifies relations of Right between persons within a state; the 'Right of Nations' pertains to relations of Right between states; and 'the Right for all nations' or 'cosmopolitan Right' concerns relations of Right between persons and foreign states" (Flikschuh 2000, 184). The normative dilemmas of political membership are to be localized within this third sphere of *jus cosmopoliticum*.

"Perpetual Peace" and cosmopolitan right – a contemporary reevaluation

Written in 1795, upon the signing of the Treaty of Basel by Prussia and revolutionary France, Kant's essay on "Perpetual Peace" has enjoyed considerable revival of attention in recent years (see Bohman and Lutz-Bachmann 1997). What makes this essay particularly interesting under the current conditions of political globalization is the visionary depth of Kant's project for perpetual peace among nations. Kant formulates three "definitive articles for perpetual peace among states." These read: "The Civil Constitution of Every State shall be Republican"; "The Law of Nations shall be founded on a Federation of Free States"; and "The Law of World Citizenship Shall be Limited to Conditions of Universal Hospitality" (Kant [1795] 1923, 434–446; [1795] 1994: 99–108).[1] Much scholarship on this essay has focused on the precise legal and political form that these articles could or would take, and on whether Kant meant to propose the establishment of a world federation of republics (*eine föderative Vereinigung*) or a league of sovereign nation-states (*Völkerbund*).

What remains frequently uncommented upon is the Third Article of "Perpetual Peace," the only one in fact that Kant himself explicitly designates with the terminology of the *Weltbürgerrecht*. The German reads: "Das Weltbürgerrecht soll auf Bedingungen der allgemeinen Hospitalität eingeschränkt sein" (Kant [1795] 1923, 443). Kant himself notes the oddity of the locution of "hospitality" in this context, and therefore remarks that "it is not a question of philanthropy but of right." In other words, hospitality is not to be understood as a virtue of sociability, as the kindness and generosity one may show to strangers who come to one's land or who become dependent upon one's acts of kindness through circumstances of nature or history; hospitality is a "right" which belongs to all human beings insofar as we view them as potential participants in a world republic. But the "right" of hospitality is

[1] I have consulted several English translations of Kant's "Perpetual Peace" essay, amending the text when necessary. For further information on these various editions, please consult the bibliography. The first date and page number refer to the German text, and the second to the English editions.

odd in that it does not regulate relationships among individuals who are members of a specific civil entity under whose jurisdiction they stand; this "right" regulates the interactions of individuals who belong to different civic entities yet who encounter one another at the margins of bounded communities. The right of hospitality is situated at the boundaries of the polity; it delimits civic space by regulating relations among members and strangers. Hence the right of hospitality occupies that space between human rights and civil rights, between the right of humanity in our person and the rights that accrue to us insofar as we are members of specific republics. Kant writes: "Hospitality [*Wirtbarkeit*] means the right of a stranger not to be treated as an enemy when he arrives in the land of another. One may refuse to receive him when this can be done without causing his destruction; but, so long as he peacefully occupies his place, one may not treat him with hostility. It is not the right to be a permanent visitor [*Gastrecht*] that one may demand. A special contract of beneficence [*ein . . . wohltätiger Vertrag*] would be needed in order to give an outsider a right to become a fellow inhabitant [*Hausgenossen*] for a certain length of time. It is only a right of temporary sojourn [*ein Besuchsrecht*], a right to associate, which all men have. They have it by virtue of their common possession [*das Recht des gemeinschaftlichen Besitzes*] of the surface of the earth, where, as a globe, they cannot infinitely disperse and hence must finally tolerate the presence of each other" (Kant [1795] 1923, 443; cf. 1949, 320).

Kant distinguishes the "right to be a permanent visitor," which he calls *Gastrecht*, from the "temporary right of sojourn" (*Besuchsrecht*). The right to be a permanent visitor is awarded through a freely chosen special agreement which goes beyond what is owed to the other morally and what he is entitled to legally; therefore, Kant names this a *wohltätiger Vertrag*, a "contract of beneficence." It is a special privilege which the republican sovereign can award to certain foreigners who abide in their territories, who perform certain functions, who represent their respective political entities, who engage in long-term trade, and the like. The *droit d'aubaine* in pre-revolutionary France, which granted foreigners certain rights of residency, the acquisition of property, and the practicing of a profession, would be a pertinent historical example. The special trade concessions that the Ottoman empire, China, Japan, and India granted westerners from the eighteenth century onward would be others. The Jews in premodern Europe, who after their persecution through the Inquisition in Spain in the fifteenth century, spread to the north, to Holland, Britain, Germany, and other territories, would be another major group to whose status both the right of hospitality and that of permanent visitorship would apply.

The right of hospitality entails a claim to temporary residency which cannot be refused, if such refusal would involve the destruction – Kant's word here is *Untergang* – of the other. To refuse sojourn to victims of religious wars, to victims of piracy or ship-wreckage, when such refusal would lead to their demise, is untenable, Kant writes. What is unclear in Kant's discussion is whether such relations among peoples and nations involve acts of supererogation, going beyond the call of moral duty, or whether they entail a certain sort of moral claim concerning the recognition of "the rights of humanity in the person of the other."

We may see here the juridical and moral ambivalence that affects discussions of the right of asylum and refuge to this day. Are the rights of asylum and refuge "rights" in the sense of being *reciprocal moral obligations* which, in some sense or another, are grounded upon our mutual humanity? Or are these rights claims in the legal sense of being *enforceable norms* of behavior which individuals and groups can hold each other to and, in particular, force sovereign nation-states to comply with? Kant's construction provides no clear answer. The right of hospitality entails a moral claim with potential legal consequences in that the obligation of the receiving states to grant temporary residency to foreigners is anchored in a republican cosmopolitical order. Such an order does not have a supreme executive law governing it. In this sense the obligation to show hospitality to foreigners and strangers cannot be enforced; it remains a voluntarily incurred obligation of the political sovereign. The right of hospitality expresses all the dilemmas of a republican cosmopolitical order in a nutshell: namely how to create quasi-legally binding obligations through voluntary commitments and in the absence of an overwhelming sovereign power with the ultimate right of enforcement.

But what exactly is Kant's justification for the "temporary right of sojourn"? Why does this claim bind the will of the republican sovereign? When reflecting on the "temporary right of sojourn" (*Besuchsrecht*), Kant uses two different premises. One premise justifies the right of temporary sojourn on the basis of the capacity of all human beings (*allen Menschen*) to associate – the German reads *sich zur Gesellschaft anzubieten* (Kant [1795] 1923, 443). The other premise resorts to the juridical construct of a "common possession of the surface of the earth" (*gemeinschaftlichen Besitzes der Oberfläche der Erde*) (ibid.). With respect to the second principle, Kant suggests that to deny the foreigner and the stranger the claim to enjoy the land and its resources, when this can be done peacefully and without endangering the life and welfare of original inhabitants, would be unjust.

The juridical construct of a purported common possession of the earth, which has a long and honorable antecedent in old European jurisprudence, functions as a double-edged sword in this context. On the one hand, Kant wants to avoid the justificatory use of this construct to legitimize western colonialist expansion; on the other hand, he wants to base the right of human beings to enter into civil association with one another upon the claim that, since the surface of the earth is limited, at some point or other, we must learn to enjoy its resources in common with others.

To understand the first of Kant's worries, recall here John Locke's argument in *The Second Treatise of Civil Government.* "In the beginning God gave the earth to men in common to enjoy" (Locke [1690] 1980, 19). The earth is a *res nullius*, belonging to all and none until it is appropriated; but to argue that the earth is a common possession of all human beings is, in effect, to disregard property relations historically existing among communities that have already settled on the land. The justification of the claim to property thus shifts from the historical title that legitimizes it to the modes of appropriation whereby what commonly belongs to a community can then be appropriated as "mine" or "thine."

Through a patently circular argument, Locke maintains that private property emerges through the fact that the means of appropriation are themselves *private*: "the labor of his body, and the work of his hands, we may say, are properly his . . . this nobody has any right to but himself" (ibid.). In the context of European expansion to the Americas in the seventeenth century, Locke's argument served to justify the colonial appropriation of the land precisely with the claim that the earth, being given to all "in common," could then be justifiably appropriated by the industrious and the thrifty, without harming existing inhabitants and, in fact, for the benefit of all (Tully 1993).

Kant explicitly rejects the *res nullius* thesis in its Lockean form, seeing in it a thinly disguised formula for expropriating non-European peoples who do not have the capacity to resist imperialist onslaughts (Kant [1795] 1994, 107; see also Muthu, 1999, 2000). He supports the Chinese and the Japanese in their attempt to keep European traders at a distance. What does the premise of the "common possession of the earth" really justify, then? Once the earth has been appropriated, others no longer have a claim to possess it. Existing property relations must be respected. If so, every community has the right to defend itself against those who seek access to its territories. Apart from the assurance that turning away the ones who seek hospitality would not cause "their destruction" – admittedly itself a vague formulation – the dire needs of others do not constitute sufficient grounds to bend the will of existing sovereign communities. The claim to the "common possession of the earth" does disappointingly little to explicate the basis of cosmopolitan right.

The sphericality of the earth and cosmopolitan right

In *Kant and Modern Political Philosophy*, Katrin Flikschuh argues that the original common possession of the earth, and in particular the limited spherical character of the earth (*der Erdkugel*), plays a much more fundamental role in Kant's justification in cosmopolitan right than I am claiming that it does. Flikschuh's argument is worth considering in some detail. Flikschuh bases this reading not on Kant's "Perpetual Peace" essay but on his *Rechtslehre*, the first half of *Die Metaphysik der Sitten* (*The Metaphysics of Morals*). Two passages are of special relevance here:

> The spherical surface of the earth unites all the places on its surface; for if its surface were an unbounded plane, men could be so dispersed on it that they would not come into any community with one another, and community would then not be a necessary result of their existence on the earth. (Kant [1797] 1922, 66; as quoted in Flikschuh 2000, 133)[2]

> Since the earth's surface is not unlimited but closed, the concepts of the Right of a state and of a Right of nations lead inevitably to the Idea *of a Right for all nations (ius gentium) or cosmopolitan Right (ius cosmopoliticum)*. So if the principle of outer freedom limited by law is lacking in any of these three possible forms of rightful condition, the framework for all others is unavoidably underdetermined

[2] Since there are some subtle discrepancies between various English editions and Flikschuh's translations, I have kept references to her versions of the relevant passages.

and must finally collapse. (Kant, [1797] 1922, 117–118; as quoted in Flikschuh 2000, 179)

Without delving into details of discrepancies which may exist between the "Perpetual Peace" essay and Kant's more difficult and fuller discussion in *The Metaphysical Elements of Justice*, for my purposes the most important question is this: does Kant mean to derive or deduce cosmopolitan right from the *fact* of the sphericality of the earth's surface? What is the status of this *fact* in Kant's moral argument? If indeed we were to assume that Kant used the sphericality of the earth as a *justificatory premise*, wouldn't we then have to conclude that he had committed the naturalistic fallacy? Just because all castles everywhere are built on sand, it still does not follow that mine should be so built as well. Likewise, just because I must, somewhere and at some point, come into contact with other human beings and cannot flee them forever, this does not imply that upon such contact I must treat them with the respect and dignity to be accorded every human being.

Flikschuh does not maintain in fact that the sphericality of the earth's surface is a justificatory premise: "The earth's spherical surface is that empirical given space for possible agency within which human beings are constrained to articulate their claims to freedom of choice and action ... To the contrary, the global boundary constitutes an objective given, unavoidable condition of empirical reality within the limits of which human agents are constrained to establish possible relations of Right" (2000, 133). The spherical surface of the earth constitutes a *circumstance of justice* but does not function as a moral justificatory premise to ground cosmopolitan right.

33

"Circumstances of justice" define indeed "the conditions of our possible agency," as Flikschuh observes. Just as the *facts* that we are all mortal beings, physically members of the same species and afflicted by similar basic needs to assure our survival constitute constraining conditions in our reasoning about justice, so too the sphericality of the earth's surface functions for Kant as a limiting condition of "outer freedom." This, I think, is amply clear from Kant's phrase, "So if the principle of outer freedom limited by law is lacking in any of these three possible forms of rightful condition . . ." (Kant [1797] 1922, 118). The "principle of outer freedom" is the justificatory premise in the argument which leads to the establishment of cosmopolitan right. Since, however, exercising our external freedom means that sooner or later, under certain circumstances, we will need to cross boundaries and come into contact with fellow human beings from other lands and cultures, we need to recognize the following: first, that the earth's surface will be apportioned into the territory of individual republics;[3] second, that conditions of right regulating intra- as well as interrepublican transactions

---

[3] I am foregoing here a consideration of the considerable difficulties of Kant's justification of property rights. Kant's dilemma appears to have been the justification of the *private* apportionment of the earth's surface without recourse to *originary acts of occupation*, since the latter, in Kant's view, establish not a condition of *right* but rather of *might*. Nevertheless, Kant finds it necessary to resort to such an argument. "This postulate can be called a permissive principle [*lex permissiva*] of practical reason, which gives us authorization that could not be got from mere concept of Right as such, namely to put all others under an obligation which they would not otherwise have, to refrain from using certain objects of our choice because we have been the first to take them into our possession" (Kant [1797] 1922, 49). The *lex permissiva* holds not only within individual republics but also *across* republics. In the light of this stipulation, we also

are necessary; and finally that among those conditions are those pertaining to the rights of hospitality and temporary sojourn. In the next chapter I hope to show that a reconstruction of the Kantian concept of the right to external freedom would lead to a more extensive system of cosmopolitan right than Kant himself offered us.

The contemporary relevance of Kant's concept of "temporary sojourn"

Kant's claim that first entry cannot be denied to those who seek it if this would result in their "destruction" (*Untergang*) has become incorporated into the Geneva Convention on the Status of Refugees as the principle of "non-refoulement" (United Nations 1951). This principle obliges signatory states not to forcibly return refugees and asylum seekers to their countries of origin if doing so would pose a clear danger to their lives and freedom. Of course, just as sovereign states can manipulate this article to define life and freedom more or less narrowly when it fits their purposes, it is also possible to circumvent the "non-refoulement" clause by depositing refugees and asylees in so-called safe third countries. Kant's formulations clearly foresaw as well as justified such balancing acts as between the moral obligations of states to those who seek refuge in their midst and

see that the claim that only the republican sovereign can grant permanent visitation rights is based on *the right of the republican sovereign to control "privately" a portion of the "common possession" of the earth's surface.* Bounded territoriality is thus made a precondition of the exercise of external freedom by Kant. Indeed, the recognition of "rightful borders" is essential if perpetual peace among nations is ever to be achieved.

to their own welfare and interests. The lexical ordering of the two claims – the moral needs of others versus legitimate self-interest – is vague, except in the most obvious cases when the life and limb of refugees would be endangered by denying them the right of entry; apart from such cases, however, the obligation to respect the liberty and welfare of the guest can permit a narrow interpretation on the part of the sovereign to whom it is addressed, and need not be considered an unconditional duty.

The universal right to hospitality which is due to every human person imposes upon us an *imperfect moral duty* to help and offer shelter to those whose life, limb, and well-being are endangered. This duty is "imperfect" – i.e., *conditional* – in that it can permit exceptions, and can be overridden by legitimate grounds of self-preservation. There is no obligation to shelter the other when doing so would endanger one's own life and limb. It is disputed in moral philosophy as to how widely or narrowly the obligation to the other should be interpreted,[4] and it is equally controversial how we should understand legitimate grounds of self-preservation: is it morally permissible to turn the needy away because we think that they are altering our cultural mores? Does the preservation of culture constitute a legitimate basis of self-preservation? Is it morally permissible

---

[4] Cf. Henry Sidgwick: ". . . but those who are in distress or urgent need have a claim on us for special kindness. These are generally recognized claims: but we find considerable difficulty and divergence, when we attempt to determine more precisely their extent and relative obligation: and the divergence becomes indefinitely greater when we compare the customs and common opinions now existing among ourselves in respect of such claims, with those of other ages and countries" (Sidgwick [1874] 1962, 246). For some recent treatments, see O'Neill 1996; Sheffler 2001.

to deny asylum when admitting large numbers of needy peoples into our territories would cause a decline in our standards of living? And what amount of decline in welfare is morally permissible before it can be invoked as grounds for denying entry to the persecuted, the needy, and the oppressed? In formulating their refugee and asylum policies, governments often implicitly utilize this distinction between perfect and imperfect duties, while human rights groups, as well as advocates of asylees and refugees, are concerned to show that the obligation to show hospitality to those in dire need should not be compromised by self-regarding interests alone. In chapter 3 I shall return to the question of obligations across borders and argue that the construal of such obligations in the light of the narrow dichotomy of legitimate self-preservation versus the duties to others is inadequate. The international system of peoples and states is characterized by such extensive interdependencies and the historical crisscrossing of fates and fortunes that the scope of special as well as generalized moral obligations to our fellow human beings far transcends the perspective of the territorially bounded state-centric system. Instead, I shall defend the perspective of a world society as the correct vantage point from which to reason about obligations across borders.

It may be objected that such criticisms of Kant are anachronistic, for what motivates Kant's formulations of cosmopolitan right are not concerns for the needs of the poor, the downtrodden, the persecuted, and the oppressed as they search for safe haven, but rather the Enlightenment preoccupation of Europeans to seek contact with other peoples and to appropriate the riches of other parts of the world. The right to seek human association, or in the literal translation of the

German, "to offer oneself to civil association [*Gesellschaft*] with others," and to seek "approach" – *Zugang* – rather than entry – *Eingang* – is for Kant a fundamental human right. This is to be distinguished from the *res nullius* thesis; in fact, the right to seek human association is at the core of what it means to be a *Weltbürger*. In true Enlightenment fashion, Kant celebrates the ship and the camel ("the desert ship," as he calls the latter) for reducing distances, breaking down barriers among local communities, and bringing the human race together. To deny "the possibility of seeking to communicate with prior inhabitants," or *ein Verkehr zu suchen* (Kant [1795] 1923, 444; 1949, 321), is contrary to cosmopolitan right. The terminology of *Verkehr zu suchen*, which can extend to commercial as well as religious, cultural, and financial contacts, betrays Kant's hope that, even if the motives of western powers in seeking to encompass the face of the globe may be less than laudatory, through increased contacts with other peoples and culture, "the human race can gradually be brought closer and closer to a cosmopolitan constitution" (*eine weltbürgerliche Verfassung*) (Kant [1795] 1923, 444; [1795] 1994, 106).

While Kant's focus fell, for understandable historical reasons, upon the right of temporary sojourn, my concern is with the unbridgeable gap he suggests exists between the right of temporary sojourn and permanent residency. The first is a right, the second a privilege; granting the first to strangers is an obligation for a republican sovereign, whereas allowing the second is a "contract of beneficence." The rights of strangers and foreigners do not extend beyond the peaceful pursuit of their means of livelihood upon the territory of another. What about the right to political membership, then? Under what conditions, if any, can the guest become a member of the republican sovereign? How are the boundaries of the sovereign defined? Kant envisages a world condition in which all members of the human race become participants in a civil order and enter into a condition of lawful association with one another. Yet this civil condition of lawful coexistence is not equivalent to membership in a republican polity. Kant's cosmopolitan citizens still need their individual republics to be citizens at all. This is why Kant is so careful to distinguish a "world government" from a "world federation." A "world government," which he argues would result only in a "universal monarchy," would be a "soulless despotism," whereas a federative union (*eine föderative Vereinigung*) would still permit the exercise of citizenship within bounded communities (Kant [1795] 1923, 453; 1949, 328).[5]

We are left with an ambiguous Kantian legacy: while liberals attempt to expand the circumstances to which first-admittance obligations would apply by building more conditions into the phrase "the destruction of the other," such as economic welfare considerations (see Kleingeld 1998, 79–85), civic republicans and defenders of national sovereignty point to Kant's condemnation of world government, as well as to his insistence upon the prerogative of the sovereign to grant membership, in order to justify the rights of national states to

---

[5] See Istvan Hont's prescient remarks: "If the 'crisis of nation-states' is linked to a weakness in the legitimation of their territorial specification, and that is linked to the legitimation of their national property in land, then the idea of the 'nation-state' cannot be *now* in crisis, because it has always been in 'crisis.' The only possible world of territorial security is the world of perpetual peace" (Hont 1995, 176).

police their borders (Martens 1996, 337–339). Kant wanted to justify the expansion of commercial and maritime capitalism in his time, insofar as these developments brought the human race into closer contact, without condoning European imperialism. The cosmopolitan right of hospitality gives one the right of peaceful temporary sojourn, but it does not entitle one to plunder and exploit, conquer and overwhelm by superior force those among whom one is seeking sojourn. Yet the cosmopolitan right is a right precisely because it is grounded upon the common humanity of each and every person and his or her freedom of will which also includes the freedom to travel beyond the confines of one's cultural, religious, and ethnocentric walls.

The Kantian cosmopolitan legacy

Kant's construction and justification of the cosmopolitan right of temporary sojourn will form a reference point for much of the following discussion. Kant's "Perpetual Peace" essay signaled a watershed between two conceptions of sovereignty and paved the way for the transition from the first to the second. We can name these "Westphalian sovereignty" and "liberal international sovereignty" (see Held 2002, 4–6; Krasner 1999, 20–25). In the classical Westphalian regime of sovereignty, states are free and equal; they enjoy ultimate authority over all objects and subjects within a circumscribed territory; relations with other sovereigns are voluntary and contingent and limited in kind and scope to transitory military and economic alliances as well as cultural and religious affinities; above all, states "regard cross-border processes as a 'private matter' concerning only those immediately affected" (Held 2002, 4).

By contrast, in conceptions of liberal international sovereignty, the formal equality of states is increasingly dependent upon their subscribing to common values and principles such as the observance of human rights and the rule of law and respect for democratic self-determination. Sovereignty no longer means ultimate and arbitrary authority; states that treat their citizens in violation of certain norms, that close borders, prevent a free market, limit freedom of speech and association, and the like, are thought not to belong within a specific society of states or alliances; the anchoring of domestic principles in institutions shared with others is crucial.

Insofar as Article One of Kant's "Perpetual Peace" reads that "The Civil Constitution of Every State shall be Republican," Kant certainly can be seen to straddle the classical Westphalian and the liberal-international models of sovereignty. The demand that the constitutions of free and equal states should be republican imposes on these states the three conditions of republican government: (1) freedom for all members of a society (as men); (2) the dependence of everyone upon a single common legislation (as subjects); (3) the principle of legal equality for everyone (as citizens) (Kant [1795] 1923, 434–443; [1795] 1994, 99–105). Whatever its precise political form may be, the league of nations – *das Völkerbund* – envisaged by Kant is first and foremost an alliance among sovereign republics which subscribe to these principles.

Kant does not go so far as to make the recognition of the sovereignty of a state depend upon its internal constitution. Nor would Kant approve "humanitarian interventions" designed to spread progressive ideals, except in one case: namely civil war and the dissolution of existing authority. This is the fifth of Kant's "preliminary articles of perpetual peace between states" (Kant [1795] 1923, 430; [1795] 1994, 96). Kant's liberalism is also less robust than our more universalist contemporary understanding in that women, domestic servants, and propertyless apprentices are named by Kant "auxiliaries to the commonwealth," and their legal status is made dependent upon the male head of household. Nevertheless, in stipulating that a republican constitution "is the original basis of every kind of civil constitution" (Kant [1795] 1923, 435; [1795] 1994, 100), and in linking peace among states to their internal constitutions, Kant paved the way from Westphalian to a liberal understanding of sovereignty. It is also remarkable that crossborder relationships which arise out of the needs of travelers, discoverers, refugees, and asylees were accorded such a significant role in delineating cosmopolitan right.

Kant clearly demarcated the tensions between the injunctions of a universalistic morality to offer temporary sojourn to all and the legal prerogative of the republican sovereign not to extend such temporary sojourn to full membership. Contra Kant, I will argue that the right to membership of the temporary resident must be viewed as a human right which can be justified along the principles of a universalistic morality. The terms and conditions under which long-term membership can be granted remain the prerogative of the republican sovereign. Yet here too human rights constraints such as non-discrimination, the right of the immigrant to due process, must be respected. While the prerogative of states to stipulate some criteria of incorporation cannot be rejected, we have to ask: which are those incorporation practices that would be *impermissible* from a moral standpoint and which are those practices that are morally *indifferent* – that is to say, neutral from the moral point of view?

Kant's formulations permit us to capture the structural contradictions between universalist and republican ideals of sovereignty in the modern revolutionary period. In conclusion, I want to name this contradiction "the paradox of democratic legitimacy" and delineate it systematically.

The paradox of democratic legitimacy

Ideally, democratic rule means that all members of a sovereign body are to be respected as bearers of human rights, and that the consociates of this sovereign freely associate with one another to establish a regime of self-governance under which each is to be considered both author of the laws and subject to them. This ideal of the original contract, as formulated by Jean-Jacques Rousseau and adopted by Kant, is a heuristically useful device for capturing the logic of modern democracies. Modern democracies, unlike their ancient counterparts, conceive of their citizens as rights-bearing consociates. The rights of the citizens rest upon the "rights of man." *Les droits de l'homme et de citoyen* do not contradict one another; quite to the contrary, they are coimplicated. This is the idealized logic of the modern democratic revolutions following the American and French examples.

The democratic sovereign draws its legitimacy not merely from its act of constitution but, equally significantly, from the conformity of this act to universal principles of human rights that are in some sense said to precede and antedate the will of the sovereign and in accordance with which the sovereign undertakes to bind itself. "We, the people," refers to a particular human community, circumscribed in space and time, sharing a particular culture, history, and legacy; yet this people establishes itself as a democratic body by acting in the name of the "universal." The tension between universal human rights claims, and particularistic cultural and national identities, is constitutive of democratic legitimacy. Modern democracies act in the name of universal principles which are then circumscribed within a particular civic community. This is the "Janus face of the modern nation," in the words of Jürgen Habermas (Habermas 1998, 115).

Since Rousseau, however, we also know that the will of the democratic people may be legitimate but unjust, unanimous but unwise. "The general will" and "the will of all" may not overlap either in theory or in practice. Democratic rule and the claims of justice may contradict one another. The democratic precommitments expressed in the idealized allegiance to universal human rights – life, liberty, and property – need to be reactualized and renegotiated within actual polities as democratic intentions. Potentially, there is always a conflict between an interpretation of these rights claims which precedes the declared formulations of the sovereign, and the actual enactments of the democratic people which could potentially violate such interpretations. We encounter this conflict in the history of political thought as the conflict between liberalism

and democracy, and even as the conflict between constitutionalism and popular sovereignty. In each case the logic of the
conflict is the same: to assure that the democratic sovereign
will uphold certain constraints upon its will by virtue of its
precommitment to certain formal and substantive interpretation of rights. Liberal and democratic theorists disagree with
one another as to the proper balance of this mix: while strong
liberals want to bind the sovereign will through precommitments to a list of human rights, strong democrats reject such a
prepolitical understanding of rights and argue that they must
be open to renegotiation and reinterpretation by the sovereign
people – admittedly within certain limits.

Yet this paradox of democratic legitimacy has a corol-
lary which has been little noted: every act of self-legislation is
also an act of self-constitution. "We, the people," who agree to
bind ourselves by these laws, are also defining ourselves as a
"we" in the very act of self-legislation. It is not only the general
laws of self-government which are articulated in this process;
the community that binds itself by these laws defines itself by
drawing boundaries as well, and these boundaries are territorial as well as civic. The will of the democratic sovereign can
extend only over the territory under its jurisdiction; democracies require borders. Empires have frontiers, while democracies have borders. Democratic rule, unlike imperial dominion,
is exercised in the name of some specific constituency and
binds that constituency alone. Therefore, at the same time that
the sovereign defines itself territorially, it also defines itself in
civic terms. Those who are full members of the sovereign body
are distinguished from those who "fall under its protection,"
but who do not enjoy "full membership rights." Women and

slaves, servants, and propertyless white males, non-Christians and non-white races, were historically excluded from membership in the sovereign body and from the project of citizenship. They were, in Kant's famous words, mere "auxiliaries to the commonwealth" (Kant [1797] 1922, 121; [1797] 1994, 140).

The boundaries of the civil community are of two kinds: on the one hand, these boundaries define the status of those who hold second-class citizenship status within the polity but who can be considered members of the sovereign people by virtue of cultural, familial, and religious attachments. Women, as well as non-propertied males before the extension of universal suffrage, fell into this category; the status of these groups is distinct from that of other residents who not only have second-class status but who also do not belong to the sovereign people by virtue of relevant identity-based criteria. Such was the status of African-American slaves until after the American Civil War and the declaration in 1865 of the 14th Amendment to the US Constitution (adopted in 1868) which conferred US citizenship upon Black peoples; such was also the status of American Indians who were granted tribal sovereignty. The status of those of Jewish faith in the original thirteen colonies that formed the United States can be described as one of transition from being an "auxiliary to the commonwealth" to being a full-fledged citizen.

In addition to these groups are those residents of the commonwealth who do not enjoy full citizenship rights either because they do not possess the requisite identity criteria through which the people defines itself, or because they belong to some other commonwealth, or because they choose to remain outsiders. These are the "aliens" and "foreigners" amidst the democratic people. Their status is distinct from that of second-class citizens such as women and workers, as well as from that of slaves and tribal peoples. This status is governed by mutual treaties among sovereign entities, as would be the case with official representatives of a state power upon the territory of the other; and if they are civilians, and live among citizens for economic, religious, or other cultural reasons, their rights and claims exist in that murky space defined by respect for human rights on the one hand and by international customary law on the other. They are refugees from religious persecution, merchants and missionaries, migrants and adventurers, explorers and fortune-seekers.

I have circumscribed in general theoretical terms the paradox of democratic legitimacy. The paradox is that the republican sovereign should undertake to bind its will by a series of precommitments to a set of formal and substantive norms, usually referred to as "human rights." The rights and claims of others – be they "auxiliaries to the commonwealth," as women, slaves, and propertyless males were considered to be, or be they subjugated peoples or foreigners – are then negotiated upon this terrain flanked by human rights on the one hand and sovereignty assertions on the other.

In what follows I will argue that, while this paradox can never be fully resolved for democracies, its impact can be mitigated through a renegotiation and reiteration of the dual commitments to human rights and sovereign self-determination. Popular sovereignty, which means that those who are subject to the law are also its authors, is not identical with territorial sovereignty. While the *demos*, as the popular sovereign, must assert control over a specific territorial domain, it can also engage in reflexive acts of self-constitution, whereby the boundaries of the *demos* can be readjusted. The politics of membership in the age of the disaggregation of citizenship rights is about negotiating the complexities of full membership rights, democratic voice, and territorial residence.

2

"The right to have rights": Hannah Arendt on the contradictions of the nation-state

The previous chapter analyzed Kant's formulation and defense of cosmopolitan right and argued that the text left unclear which of the following premises justified the cosmopolitan right to hospitality: the right to seek human association, which in fact, could be viewed as an extension of the human claim to freedom; or the premise of the sphericity of the earth's surface and the juridical fiction of the common possession of the earth. Kant's discussion of cosmopolitan right, whatever its shortcomings, delineates a new terrain in the history of political thought. In formulating a sphere of right – in the juridical and moral senses of the term – between domestic constitutional and customary international law, Kant charted a terrain onto which the nations of this world began to venture only at the end two world wars. Kant was concerned that the granting of the right to permanent residency (*Gastrecht*) should remain a privilege of self-governing republican communities. Naturalization is a sovereign privilege. The obverse side of naturalization is "denationalization," or loss of citizenship status.

After Kant, it was Hannah Arendt who turned to the ambiguous legacy of cosmopolitan law, and who dissected the paradoxes at the heart of the territorially based sovereign state system. One of the great political thinkers of the twentieth century, Hannah Arendt argued that the twin phenomena

49

of "political evil" and "statelessness" would remain the most daunting problems into the twenty-first century as well (Arendt 1994, 134; [1951] 1968; see Benhabib [1996] 2003). Arendt always insisted that among the root causes of totalitarianism was the collapse of the nation-state system in Europe during the two world wars. The totalitarian disregard for human life and the eventual treatment of human beings as "superfluous" entities began, for Hannah Arendt, when millions of human beings were rendered "stateless" and denied the "right to have rights." Statelessness, or the loss of nationality status, she argued, was tantamount to the loss of all rights. The stateless were deprived not only of their citizenship rights; they were deprived of any human rights. The rights of man and the rights of the citizen, which the modern bourgeois revolutions had so clearly delineated, were deeply imbricated. The loss of citizenship rights, therefore, contrary to all human rights declarations, was politically tantamount to the loss of human rights altogether.

This chapter begins with an examination of Arendt's contribution; thereafter, I develop a series of systematic considerations which are aimed to show why neither the right to naturalization nor the prerogative of denaturalization can be considered sovereign privileges alone; the first is a universal human right, while the second – denaturalization – is its abrogation.

Imperialism and the "End of the Rights of Man"

In *The Origins of Totalitarianism*, first published in Britain in 1951 as *The Burden of Our Times*, Arendt wrote:

Something much more fundamental than freedom and justice, which are rights of citizens, is at stake when belonging to a community into which one is born is no longer a matter of course and not belonging no longer a matter of choice, or when one is placed in a situation where, unless he commits a crime, his treatment by others does not depend on what he does or does not do. This extremity, and nothing else, is the situation of people deprived of human rights. They are deprived, not of the right to freedom, but of the right to action; not of the right to think whatever they please, but of the right to opinion ... *We become aware of the existence of a right to have rights (and that means to live in a framework where one is judged by one's actions and opinions) and a right to belong to some kind of organized community, only when millions of people emerge who had lost and could not regain these rights because of the new global political situation.* (Arendt [1951] 1968, 177. My emphasis.)

The phrase "the right to have rights" and Arendt's resounding plea for the acknowledgment of the right of every human being to "belong to some community" are introduced at the end of part II of *The Origins of Totalitarianism*, which is called "Imperialism." To understand Arendt's philosophical intentions, it is necessary to follow the broad outlines of this discussion. In the opening sections of "Imperialism," Arendt examines the European "scramble for Africa." Her thesis is that the encounter with Africa allowed the colonizing white nations such as the Belgians, the Dutch, the British, the Germans, and the French to transgress abroad those moral limits that would normally control the exercise of power at home. In the encounter with Africa, civilized white men regressed to levels of inhumanity by plundering, looting, burning, and raping the "savages" whom they encountered. Arendt uses Joseph Conrad's famous story, "The Heart of Darkness," as a parable of this encounter. The "heart of darkness" is not in Africa alone; twentieth-century totalitarianism brings this center of darkness to the European continent itself. The lessons learned in Africa seem to be practiced in the heart of Europe.

Arendt's attempt to locate in the European scramble for Africa some distant source of European totalitarianism, and in particular of racial-extermination policies, is brilliant, although it remains historically as well as philosophically underexplored. Throughout this discussion she examines distinct historical episodes as illustrating the breakdown of the rule of law: the destruction of the ideal of citizens' consent through secret administrative decisions and imperialist manipulations, as in the case of British rule in India and French rule in Egypt; the fragility of principles of human rights to govern interactions among human beings who, in fact, have nothing but their humanity in common, as evidenced by the colonization of Africa; the instrumentalization of the nation-state for the plundering greed of the bourgeois classes, an experiment in which all major European nations more or less took part. Her discussion of imperialism, which begins with the European "scramble for Africa," concludes with "The Decline of the Nation-State and the End of the Rights of Man."

Through an analysis whose significance for contemporary developments is only too obvious after the civil wars in the former Yugoslavia in the mid-1990s, Arendt subsequently turns to the nationalities and minorities question which emerged in the wake of World War I. The dissolution of the multinational and multiethnic empires such as the Russian, the Ottoman, and the Austro-Hungarian and the defeat of the Kaiserreich led to the emergence of nation-states, particularly in the territories of east-central Europe, which enjoyed neither religious, nor linguistic, nor cultural homogeneity. The successor states of these empires – Poland, Austria, Hungary, Czechoslovakia, Yugoslavia, Bulgaria, Lithuania, Latvia, Estonia, and the Greek and the Turkish republics – controlled territories in which large numbers of so-called national minorities resided. On June 28, 1919, the Polish Minority Treaty was concluded between President Woodrow Wilson and the Allied and associated powers, to protect the rights of minorities who made up nearly 40 percent of the total population of Poland at that time and consisted of Jews, Russians, Germans, Lithuanians, and others. Thirteen similar agreements were then drawn up with various successor governments "in which they pledged to their minorities civil and political equality, cultural and economic freedom, and religious toleration" (Fink 1972, 331). Not only was there a fatal lack of clarity in how a "national minority" was to be defined, but the fact that the protection of minority rights applied only to the successor states of the defeated powers, whereas Great Britain, France, and Italy refused to consider the generalization of the minority treaties to their own territories, created cynicism about the motivations of the Allied powers in supporting minority rights in the first place (ibid., 334). This situation led to anomalies whereby, for example, the German minority in Czechoslovakia could petition the League of Nations for the protection of its rights but the large

German minority in Italy could not. The position of Jews in all successor states was also unsettled: if they were a "national minority," was it by virtue of their race, their religion, or their language that they were to be considered as such, and exactly which rights would this minority status entail? Other than the rights to the free exercise of religion and instruction in Hebrew schools, what educational and cultural rights would be granted to populations as diverse as the Austrian Jews, the Russian Jews, and the Turkish Sephardic community in the former territories of the Ottoman empire, to name but a few instances?

For Arendt, the gradual discord within and the resulting political ineptitude of the League of Nations, the emerging conflicts between so-called national minorities themselves, and the hypocrisy in the application of the minority treaties – all were harbingers of developments to come in the 1930s. The modern nation-state was being transformed from an organ which would execute the rule of law for all its citizens and residents into an instrument of the nation alone. "The nation had conquered the state, national interest had priority over law long before Hitler could pronounce 'right is what is good for the German people'" (Arendt [1951] 1968, 275).

The perversion of the modern state from being an instrument of law into one of lawless discretion in the service of the nation was completed when states began to practice massive denaturalizations against unwanted minorities, thus creating millions of refugees, deported aliens, and stateless peoples across borders. Refugees, minorities, stateless and displaced persons are special categories of human beings created through the actions of the nation-state. In a territorially bounded nation-state system, that is, in a "state-centric" international order, one's legal status is dependent upon protection by the highest authority that controls the territory upon which one resides and issues the papers to which one is entitled. One becomes a *refugee* if one is persecuted, expelled, and driven away from one's homeland; one becomes a *minority* if the political majority in the polity declares that certain groups do not belong to the supposedly "homogeneous" people; one is a *stateless person* if the state whose protection one has hitherto enjoyed withdraws such protection, as well as nullifying the papers it has granted; one is a *displaced person* if, having been once rendered a refugee, a minority, or a stateless person, one cannot find another polity to recognize one as its member, and remains in a state of limbo, caught between territories, none of which desire one to be its resident. It is here that Arendt concludes:

> We become aware of the existence of a right to have rights (and that means to live in a framework where one is judged by one's actions and opinions) and a right to belong to some kind of organized community, only when millions of people emerge who had lost and could not regain these rights because of the new global political situation . . . The right that corresponds to this loss and that was never even mentioned among the human rights cannot be expressed in the categories of the eighteenth century because they presume that rights spring immediately from the "nature" of man . . . the right to have rights, or the right of every individual to belong to humanity, should be guaranteed by humanity itself. It is by no means certain whether this is possible. (Arendt [1951] 1968, 296–297)

As Frank Michelman has observed in an illuminating essay, "Parsing 'A Right to Have Rights,'" "As matters have actually developed . . . the having of rights depends on receipt of a special sort of social recognition and acceptance – that is, of one's juridical status within some particular concrete political community. The notion of a right to have rights arises out of the modern-statist conditions and is equivalent to the moral claim of a refugee or other stateless person to citizenship, or at least juridical personhood, within the social confines of some law-dispensing state" (Michelman 1996, 203). But what kind of a moral claim is the one advanced by the refugee and the asylee, the guest worker and the immigrant, to be recognized as a member? What kind of a right is entailed in the right to have rights?

The many meanings of "the right to have rights"

Let me begin by analyzing the phrase "the right to have rights." Is the concept "right" being used in an equivalent fashion in the two halves of the phrase? Is the right to be acknowledged by others as a person who is entitled to rights in general of the same status as the rights to which one would be entitled after such recognition? Clearly not. The first use of the term "right" is addressed to humanity as such and enjoins us to recognize membership in some human group. In this sense this use of the term "right" evokes *a moral imperative*: "Treat all human beings as persons belonging to some human group and entitled to the protection of the same." What is invoked here is a *moral claim to membership* and *a certain form of treatment compatible with the claim to membership*.

56

The second use of the term "right" in the phrase "the right to have rights" is built upon this prior claim of membership. To have a right, when one is already a member of an organized political and legal community, means that "I have a claim to do or not to do A, and you have an obligation not to hinder me from doing or not doing A." Rights claims entitle persons to engage or not in a course of action, and such entitlements create reciprocal obligations. Rights and obligations are correlated: rights discourse takes place among the consociates of a community. Such rights, which generate reciprocal obligations among consociates, that is, among those who are already recognized as members of a legal community, are usually referred to as "civil and political" rights or as citizens' rights. Let us then name the second use of the term "right" in the phrase "the right to have rights" its *juridico-civil usage*. In this usage, "rights" suggests a triangular relationship between the person who is entitled to rights, others upon whom this obligation creates a duty, and the protection of this rights claim and its enforcement through some established legal organ, most commonly the state and its apparatus.

The first use of the term "right" in the phrase "the right to have rights" does not show the same discursive structure as its second use: in the first mention, the identity of the other(s) to whom the claim to be recognized as a rights-bearing person is addressed remains open and indeterminate. Note that for Arendt such recognition is first and foremost a recognition to "membership," the recognition that one "belongs" to some organized human community. One's status as a rights-bearing person is contingent upon the recognition of one's membership. Who is to give or withhold such recognition? Who are the addressees of the claim that one "should be acknowledged as a member"? Arendt's answer is clear: humanity itself; and yet she adds, "It is by no means certain whether this is possible." The asymmetry between the first and second uses of the term "right" derives from the absence in the first case of a specific juridico-civil community of consociates who stand in a relation of reciprocal duty to one another. And what would this duty be? The duty to recognize one as a member, as one who is protected by the legal-political authorities and as one who is to be treated as a person entitled to the enjoyment of rights.

This claim and the duty it imposes upon us are "moral" in the Kantian sense of the term, because they concern us as human beings as such, thus transcending all cultural, religious, and linguistic affiliations and distinctions that distinguish us from each other. Arendt, though her thinking is thoroughly Kantian, will not follow Kant. But it is important to recall Kant's arguments here.

Let us bracket for the moment Kant's justification of the categorical imperative. Let us assume that the moral law in one of its many formulations is valid and let us focus on the *Zweck an sich* (end-in-itself) principle, namely: "Act in such a way that you treat humanity in all your actions as an end, and never as a means only." For Kant, this moral law legitimizes the "right of humanity in one's person," that is, the right to be treated by others in accordance with certain standards of human dignity and worthiness. This right imposes negative duties upon us, i.e., duties which oblige us never to act in ways that would violate the right of humanity in every person. Such violation would occur first and foremost if and when we were to refuse to enter into civil society with one another, that is, if we were to refuse to become legal consociates. The right of humanity in our person imposes a reciprocal obligation on us to enter into civil society and to accept that our freedom will be limited by civil legislation, such that the freedom of one can be made compatible with the freedom of each under a universal law. The right of humanity leads Kant to justify the social contract of civil government under which we all become legal consociates (Kant [1797] 1994, 133–134). In Arendtian language, the right of humanity entitles us to become a member of civil society such that we can then be entitled to juridico-civil rights. The moral claim of the guest not to be treated with hostility upon arriving in the lands of another and his or her claim to temporary hospitality rest upon this moral injunction against violating the rights of humanity in the individual person. It is not the common possession of the earth, but rather this right of humanity, and the right to freedom which follows from it, that serves as the philosophical justification for cosmopolitan right.

Arendt herself was skeptical about such justificatory philosophical discourses, seeing in them a form of metaphysical foundationalism. For this reason, she was able to offer a political but not a conceptual solution to the problems posed by the state prerogative of denationalizations. The right to have rights, in her view, transcends the contingencies of birth which differentiate and divide us from one another. The right to have rights can be realized only in a political community in which we are judged not through the characteristics which define us at birth, but through our actions and opinions, by what we do and say and think. "Our political life," writes Arendt, "rests on the assumption that we can produce equality through organization, because man can act and change and build a common world, together with his equals and only with his equals . . . We are not born equal; we become equal as members of a group on the strength of our decision to guarantee ourselves mutually equal rights" (Arendt [1951] 1968, 301).

In contemporary terms Arendt is advocating a "civic" as opposed to an "ethnic" ideal of polity and belonging. It is the mutual recognition by a group of consociates of each other as equal rights-bearing persons that constitutes for her the true meaning of political equality. Despite its perversions through the Dreyfus affair, France, for this reason, remained for Arendt *la nation par excellence*. Could it be, then, that the institutional, even if not philosophical, solution to the dilemmas of human rights is to be found in the establishment of principles of civic nationalism? Of course, civic nationalism would entail a *jus soli*-based mode of acquiring citizenship, that is, the acquisition of citizenship rights through birth on the territory or through a citizen mother or father. *Jus sanguinis*, by contrast, means the acquisition of citizenship rights through ethnic lineage and descent alone, usually – but not always – through proof that the father was a member of a particular ethnic group. *Jus sanguinis* is based on the conflation of the *ethnos* with the *demos*, of "belonging to a people" with "membership in the state." Undoubtedly, Arendt defends an ideal of the civic nation based upon a *jus soli*-mode of citizenship acquisition. Yet her diagnosis of the tensions inherent in the ideal of the nation-state suggests that there is a deeper malaise in this institutional structure, a deeper perplexity about the "decline of the nation-state and the end of the rights of man."

To put the issue sharply: Arendt was just as skeptical about the ideals of world government as she was about the possibility of nation-state systems ever achieving justice and equality for all. World government would destroy the space for politics in that it would not allow individuals to defend shared public spaces in common (an assumption which underestimates the potentialities for planetary politics). The nation-state system, on the other hand, always carried within itself the seeds of exclusionary injustice at home and aggression abroad.

Arendt on the nation-state

It remains one of the most puzzling aspects of Hannah Arendt's political thought that, although she criticized the weaknesses of the nation-state system, she was equally skeptical about all ideals of a world government. Arendt's philosophical and political ambivalence toward the nation-states has complex dimensions. The nation-state system, established in the wake of the American and French Revolutions, and bringing to culmination processes of development at work since European absolutism in the sixteenth century, is based upon the tension, and at times outright contradiction, between human rights and the principle of national sovereignty.

The modern state has always also been a specific nation-state. This is the case even when this nationalism is civic in form, as is usually associated with the North American, French, British, and Latin American models, or ethnic, as is usually associated with the German and east-central European models. The citizens of the modern state are always also members of a nation, of a particular human group which shares a certain history, language, and tradition – however problematically this identity may be constituted.

It is in her writings on Zionism that we find the key to Arendt's critique of nationalism. In an essay published in 1945 called "Zionism Reconsidered," Arendt criticized all nationalisms, Zionism of Theodor Herzl's type not excluded, for their claim that "the nation was an eternal organic body, the product of inevitable growth of inherent qualities; it explains peoples, not in terms of political organizations, but in terms of biological superhuman personalities" (Arendt [1945] 1978, 156). For Arendt, this kind of thinking was prepolitical in its roots, because it applied metaphors drawn from the domain of prepolitical life, such as organic bodies, family unities, and blood communities, to the sphere of politics. The more that nationalist ideologies stressed aspects of identity which preceded the political, the more they based the equality of the citizens on their presumed commonality and sameness. Equality among consociates in a democratic *Rechtstaat* should be differentiated from sameness of cultural and ethnic identity. Civic equality is not sameness, but entails respect for difference.

It is important to note that after the Holocaust and the attempted extermination of European Jewry, Arendt's support for a Jewish homeland changed. Although she never accepted Zionism as the dominant cultural and political project of the Jewish people, and chose to live her life in a multinational and multicultural liberal-democratic state, the catastrophes of World War II made Arendt more appreciative of the moment of new beginning inherent in all state formations. "The restoration of human rights," she observed, "as the recent example of the State of Israel proves, has been achieved so far only through the restoration or establishment of national rights" (Arendt [1951] 1968, 299). Arendt was too knowledgeable and shrewd an observer of politics not to have also noted that the cost of the establishment of the state of Israel was the disenfranchisement of the Arab residents of Palestine, and hostility in the Middle East until the present. She hoped throughout the 1950s that a binational Jewish and Palestinian state would become a reality (see Benhabib [1996] 2003, 43–47).

What can we conclude from the historical and institutional contradictions of the idea of the nation-state? Is Arendt's begrudging acceptance of this political formation a concession to political realism and historical inevitabilities? Could Arendt be saying that no matter how contradiction-fraught the nation-state may be as an institutional structure, it is still the only one that defends the rights of all who are its citizens – at least in principle, even if not in practice?

Ironically, Arendt had a very clear understanding of the limitations of the nation-state when it aspired to become the state of a supposedly homogeneous nation. "The real goal of the Jews in Palestine," she wrote, "is the building up of a Jewish homeland. This goal must never be sacrificed to the pseudo-sovereignty of a Jewish state" (Arendt [1945] 1978, 192). Arendt distinguished the grand French idea of the "sovereignty of the people" from "the nationalist claims of autarchical existence" (ibid., 156). "People's sovereignty" refers to the democratic self-organization and political will of a people, who may or may not share the same ethnicity, but who choose to constitute themselves as a sovereign and self-legislating body politic.

This idea of popular sovereignty is distinct from nationalism, which presupposes that "the nation was an eternal organic body"(ibid.). Arendt believed that this kind of nationalism, in addition to being conceptually false, becomes most virulent when it is rendered historically obsolete: "as for nationalism, it was never more evil or more fiercely defended than since it became apparent that this once great and revolutionary principle of the national organization of peoples could no longer either guarantee true sovereignty of the people within or establish a just relationship among different peoples beyond the national borders" (ibid., 141). Arendt clearly saw that to attain true democratic sovereignty and to establish justice beyond borders, one needed to go beyond the state-centric model of the twentieth century. She hoped, against hope, that extensive local democracy, in which Jews and Arabs would participate commonly, and a federative state structure, integrated within a larger community of peoples in the Meditteranean, would flourish (see Benhabib [1996] 2003, 41–43).

Nevertheless, in her reflections on the paradoxes of the right to have rights, Arendt took the framework of the nation-state, whether in its ethnic or civic variants, as a given. Her more experimental, fluid, and open reflections on how to constitute democratically sovereign communities, which did not follow the model of the nation-state, were not explored further. I want to suggest that the experiment of the modern nation-state could be analyzed in different terms: the formation of the democratic people with its unique history and culture can be seen as an ongoing process of transformation and reflexive experimentation with collective identity in a process of democratic iterations. Here I take my cue from Arendt and

I depart from her. The contradiction between human rights and sovereignty needs to be reconceptualized as the inherently conflictual aspects of reflexive collective-identity formation in complex, and increasingly multicultural and multinational, democracies.

Kant and Arendt on rights and sovereignty

In chapter 1, I recalled at length Kant's argument concerning the cosmopolitan right to temporary sojourn. Kant clearly showed the tensions that arise between the moral obligation we owe each human being to grant them sojourn on the one hand, and the prerogative of the republican sovereign on the other not to extend this temporary right of stay to permanent membership.

We should note how close Kant and Arendt are on this score. Just as Kant leaves unexplained the philosophical and political step that could lead from the right of temporary sojourn to the right of membership, so too Arendt could not base "the right to have rights," i.e., to be recognized as a member of some organized human community, upon some further philosophical principle. For Kant, granting the right to membership remains the prerogative of the republican sovereign and involves an act of "beneficence." For Arendt, the actualization of the right to have rights entails the establishment of republican polities in which the equality of each is guaranteed by the recognition of all. Such acts of republican constitution-making transform the inequalities and exclusions among human beings into a regime of equal rights claims. Arendt herself is deeply aware of the lingering paradox that every act of republican constitution establishes new "insiders" and "outsiders." While the ark of political equality extends to protect *some*, it can never extend shelter to *all*, for then we would not have individual polities but a world state, to which Arendt is just as intensely opposed as Kant himself was.

I am arguing, then, that in Kant's as well as Arendt's work we encounter the same tension-filled conceptual construction: first and foremost are universalist moral claims concerning the obligations we owe to each other as human beings. For Kant, this is the obligation to grant refuge to each human being in need, whereas for Hannah Arendt this is the obligation not to deny membership or not to deny the right to have rights. Yet for each thinker this universalist moral right is politically and juridically so circumscribed that every act of inclusion generates its own terms of exclusion. For Kant, there is no *moral claim* to permanent residency; for Arendt, there is no escaping the historical arbitrariness of republican acts of founding whose ark of equality will always include some and exclude others. Republican equality is distinct from universal moral equality. The right to have rights cannot be guaranteed by a world state or another world organization, but only by the collective will of circumscribed polities, which in turn, willy-nilly, perpetuate their own regimes of exclusion. We may say that Arendt's and Kant's moral cosmopolitanism founders on their legal and civic particularism. The paradox of democratic self-determination leads the democratic sovereign to self-constitution as well as to exclusion.

Is there a way out of these dilemmas? Philosophically, we need to begin by taking a closer look at the two horns of this dilemma: the concept of rights on the one hand and that of sovereign privilege on the other. Their assumptions concerning republican sovereignty lead Arendt and Kant to believe that exclusionary territorial control is an unchecked sovereign privilege which cannot be limited or trumped by other norms and institutions. I want to show that this is not the case and that cosmopolitan rights create a network of obligations and imbrications around sovereignty. My argument will proceed at the conceptual as well as institutional level.

Since Arendt penned her prophetic analysis of the "Decline of the Nation-State and the End of the Rights of Man," institutional and normative developments in international law have begun to address some of the paradoxes which she and Kant were unable to resolve. When Arendt wrote that the right to have rights was a fundamental moral claim as well as an insoluble political problem, she did not mean that aliens, foreigners, and residents did not possess *any* rights. In certain circumstances, as with Jews in Germany, Greek and Armenian nationals in the period of the founding of the republic of Turkey (1923), and German refugees in Vichy France – to name but a few cases – entire groups of people were denaturalized or denationalized, and lost the protection of a sovereign legal body. For Arendt, neither the institutional nor the theoretical solution to this problem was at hand. Institutionally, several arrangements have emerged since World War II that express the learning process of the nations of this world in dealing with the horrors of this century: the 1951 Geneva Convention Relating to the Status of Refugees and its Protocol added in 1967, the creation of the UN High Commissioner on Refugees (UNHCR), and the formation of the World Court, and most recently of an International Criminal Court through the Treaty of Rome, are developments intended to protect those whose right to have rights has been denied.

Furthermore, significant developments in international law point in the direction of the *decriminalization* of migratory movements, whether these be caused by the search for refuge or asylum, or by immigration proper. The right to have rights today means the recognition of the universal status of personhood of each and every human being independently of their national citizenship. Whereas for Arendt, ultimately, citizenship was the prime guarantor for the protection of one's human rights, the challenge ahead is to develop an international regime which decouples the right to have rights from one's nationality status (see ch. 5).

Legal scholars distinguish between the juridical, social, and individualist perspectives dominant in refugee law (Hathaway 1991, 2–8). The first refugee definitions from 1920 until 1935 were formulated in response to the denial of formal protection through the state of origin. Hathaway observes that "The withdrawal of *de jure* protection by a state, whether by way of denaturalization or the withholding of diplomatic facilities such as travel documents and consular representation, results in a malfunction in the entire legal system. Because the then existing international law did not recognize individuals as subjects of international rights and obligation, the determination of responsibilities on the international plane fell to the sovereign state whose protection one enjoyed" (ibid., 3).

In response to massive denaturalizations which occurred in the interwar period in the newly established republics of Europe, the League of Nations extended protection to groups of persons whose nationality had been withdrawn from them. Also, people without passports were recognized as entitled to legal protection. This is the historical background of Arendt's considerations on statelessness. Since that time, the definition of a Convention refugee under international law has been expanded to accommodate individuals who are the helpless casualties of broadly based social or political occurrences, and assistance is offered to ensure the refugee's safety and well-being. A further set of developments in the system of international refugee protection has led to the inclusion of individuals who are in search of escape from perceived injustice or persecution in their home state. Article 14 of the Universal Declaration of Human Rights anchors the right to asylum as a universal human right. The text of the article reads: "Everyone has the right to seek and to enjoy in other countries asylum from persecution. This right may not be invoked in the case of prosecutions genuinely arising from non-political crimes or from acts contrary to the purposes and principles of the United Nations" (quoted ibid., 14). Nevertheless, while the right to seek asylum is recognized as a human right, the *obligation to grant asylum* continues to be jealously guarded by states as a sovereign privilege. In this sense, and despite considerable developments of international law in protecting the status of stateless persons, as well as of refugees and asylees, neither Kant nor Arendt were wholly wrong in singling out the conflict between universal human rights and sovereignty claims as being the root paradox at the heart of the territorially bounded state-centric international order.

3

The Law of Peoples, distributive
justice, and migrations

When at the end of the eighteenth century Kant penned his reflections on cosmopolitan right, the expansion of western imperialist ventures into the Americas had been underway for several centuries, since the late 1400s, while in the same period the Dutch, the Portuguese, the Spanish, and the British imperial navies had been vying with each other for dominance in the Indian Ocean, Southeast Asia, and the Far East. The right to hospitality was articulated against the background of such western colonial and expansionist ambitions. Kant's extensive references to the opening of Japan and China to western travelers and merchants in the "Perpetual Peace" essay give us a very lively sense of this historical context (Kant [1795] 1923, 444–446; see also Wischke 2002, 227).

Arendt's reflections on statelessness emerge against a different historical background: the collapse of the multinational and multiethnic empires in Europe in the period between two world wars. The extensive use of denaturalization – that is, revocation of citizenship rights – to deal with unwanted minorities and refugees on the part of the European nation-states emerges in this context. A most brilliant, even if not fully explored, insight on Arendt's part is that the experiences gained by western powers during the colonization of Africa

A shorter version of this chapter appeared as "The *Law of Peoples*, Distributive Justice, and Migration," in a symposium on Rawls and the Law, *Fordham Law Review*, 72(5) (April 2004), 1761–1788.

inform and even historically inspire the treatment of minorities in continental Europe. Overseas imperialism and continental imperialism are related. Despite these observations, missing from Kant's as well as Arendt's considerations is an explicit recognition of the economic interdependence of peoples in a world society. Notwithstanding their astute insights into the paradoxes of cosmopolitan right, a more robust analysis of the interdependence of peoples, nations, and states is lacking from their formulations.

Much contemporary neo-Kantian discourse on immigration, when it addresses the issue of such interdependence at all, treats it from the standpoint of distributive justice on a global scale. It is assumed that the principal grounds for migratory movements are economic, and that border-crossing movements must be viewed in the context of world economic interdependencies. Contemporary Kantian cosmopolitans treat border-crossings, whether they be those of refugees, asylees, or immigrants, within the framework of global distributive justice.

In this chapter, I examine these contemporary debates. Beginning with John Rawls's work, I argue that Rawls's Law of Peoples is state-centric and cannot do justice either sociologically or normatively to questions raised by border-crossings. Global-justice theorists, such as Thomas Pogge and Charles Beitz, go much further than Rawls in pleading for justice across borders. But they subsume migratory movements under global distributive justice. Although each party appeals to Kant, they each distort Kant's position in significant ways. I will ask: what would be the contours of cosmopolitan right in the Kantian tradition, if we proceed from the view that human migratory movements have been ubiquitous throughout human history, and that the actions of sovereign states in an interdependent world constitute "pull" as well as "push" factors in migration? My answer has several components: first, empirically I want to argue for the interdependence of peoples in a world society. Interactions among human communities are perennial and not the exception in human history. Rather, the emergence of a regime of clearly demarcated sovereign state-territoriality is itself a recent product of modernity. Second, migration rights cannot be subsumed under distributive-justice claims, and, finally, the right to membership ought to be considered a human right, in the moral sense of the term, and it ought to become a legal right as well by being incorporated into states' constitutions through citizenship and naturalization provisions.

Neo-Kantian theories of global justice have been challenged by an influential school which I shall name "the decline of citizenship." These theorists maintain that membership in cultural and political communities is not a matter of distributive justice but, rather, a crucial aspect of a community's self-understanding and self-determination. While agreeing with this claim, I take issue with the views on migration and citizenship of Michael Walzer, who is one of the foremost thinkers in this vein. Walzer, I claim, conflates ethical and political integration, in that he views the liberal-democratic state as a holistic cultural and ethical entity. I argue that it is not. While Walzer and others are right in raising concerns about the transformations of citizenship in the contemporary world, they are wrong in blaming immigration for these changes. I share their concern for democratic self-governance, but I maintain that the institutional developments of citizenship rights in the contemporary world are much more complicated and multi-faceted than communitarians and decline-of-citizenship theorists would have us believe. I characterize these transformations as the "disaggregation of citizenship" (see ch. 4).

Migrations and John Rawls's *The Law of Peoples*

Political membership – the conditions of entry and exit into societies – has rarely been considered an important aspect of theories of domestic and international justice. John Rawls's political philosophy is no exception. Thus in *Political Liberalism* Rawls writes that "a democratic society, like any political society, is to be viewed as a *complete and closed social system*. It is complete in that it is self-sufficient and has a place for all the main purposes of human life. It is also closed . . . in that entry into it is only by birth and exit from it is only by death . . . Thus, we are not seen as joining society at the age of reason, as we might join an association, but as being born into a society where we will lead a complete life" (Rawls 1993, 41. My emphasis).

Surely, Rawls meant to use the model of a closed society as a counterfactual fiction, as a convenient thought-experiment in reasoning about justice; yet, by not granting conditions of entry and exit into the political community a central role in a liberal-democratic theory of justice, he assumed that the state-centric model of territorially delimited nations, with fairly closed and well-guarded borders, would continue to govern our thinking in these matters. Rawls's reasons for choosing a state-centric perspective in reasoning about international justice were made amply clear subsequently in *The Law of Peoples.* "An important role of a people's government, however arbitrary a society's boundaries may appear from a historical point of view, is to be the representative and effective agent of a people as they take responsibility for their territory and its environmental integrity, as well as for the size of their population" (Rawls 1999, 38–39). Rawls adds in the footnote to this passage that "a people has at least a qualified right to limit immigration. I leave aside here what these qualifications might be" (ibid., 39 n. 48). In choosing bounded political communities as the relevant unit for developing a conception of domestic and international justice, Rawls was departing significantly from Immanuel Kant and his teaching of cosmopolitan law. If Kant's major advance was to articulate a domain of relations of justice which were valid for all individuals as moral persons in the international arena, in Rawls's *The Law of Peoples* individuals are not the principal agents of justice but are instead submerged into unities which Rawls names "peoples." For Kant, the essence of *jus cosmopoliticum* was the thesis that all moral persons were members of a world society in which they could potentially interact with one another. Rawls, by contrast, sees individuals as members of peoples and not as cosmopolitan citizens.

There has been considerable debate in the literature as to why Rawls would choose to develop a view of international justice from the standpoint of peoples rather than of individuals (Beitz 2000; Buchanan 2000; Kuper 2000). This methodological beginning leads him to articulate principles of international justice not for individuals, considered as units of equal moral respect and concern in a world society, but for peoples and their representatives. But the cogency of Rawls's definition of peoples is doubtful. An examination of Rawls's assumptions concerning peoples will also help us clarify why for him bounded communities are the units of an ideal theory of global justice, whereas migrations become a matter for non-ideal theory.

The concept of peoples is introduced by Rawls as a device of representation, much as the conception of the moral person was in *A Theory of Justice* ([1971] 1972) and that of the citizen was in *Political Liberalism* (1993). A device of representation accentuates certain features of the object to be represented while bracketing or minimizing others. So it is too with the concept of peoples. Rawlsian peoples are ideally defined as "liberal peoples" and have three basic features: "a reasonably just constitutional democratic government that serves their fundamental interests; citizens united by what Mill called 'common sympathies'; and finally, a moral nature" (Rawls 1999, 23). A major concern of the Rawlsian view of justice becomes how or why a Law of Peoples chosen by the representatives of liberal peoples would be acceptable to non-liberal peoples as well. Hence, the Law of Peoples is developed in two steps, first from the perspective of liberal societies and subsequently from the standpoint of "decent, non-liberal peoples" (ibid. 59–68 cf. Beitz 2000, 675).

More significant, though, is the admixture of sociological and ethical attributes of peoples in Rawls's view. Rawls's category bundles together empirical as well as normative features: while most social scientists and historians would agree that some modicum of "common sympathies" may be necessary to distinguish one people or nation from another, it is odd to stipulate that peoples would not be such unless they were governed by "a just constitutional democratic government."[1] The difficulty arises from Rawls's stringing together normative stipulations with sociological characteristics. Rawls's method of idealization makes it difficult to understand whether he intends his concept of peoples to be historically and sociologically cogent or merely normatively acceptable from the standpoint of his principles of justice. Clearly, he intends it to be both but conflating these two perspectives right at the outset creates a series of problems which reverberate throughout the subsequent argument.

Since he wishes to avoid the pitfalls of realist international theory which takes states and their interests as the principal actors in the international arena, Rawls wishes to distinguish states from peoples. He argues that peoples, not states, are the relevant moral and sociological actors in reasoning about justice on a global scale. Yet he fails to convince that an analytically viable distinction between peoples and states can be made on his own terms. What political form besides that of a modern state could a people who is to be governed by

[1] Cf. Robert H. Wiebe's definition: "Nationalism is the desire among people *who believe they share a common ancestry and a common destiny* to live under their own government on land sacred to their history. Nationalism expresses an aspiration with a political objective" (2002, 5). Note how this definition finesses the question of whether people actually share a common ancestry or destiny; that they believe that they do is what is important for nationalist movements. But the social scientist need not share this belief, although he reckons with it as a crucial factor in understanding nationalism. Such a duality of perspectives, as between social actors and social observers, is absent from Rawls's definition of peoplehood altogether.

"a just constitutional democratic government" possess? Could this be an empire? Could this be a city-state?

Rawls insists that peoples are not states principally because he does not wish to ascribe them sovereignty. Two of the most commonly associated features of sovereignty, namely internal sovereignty over a population and external sovereignty to declare war against other sovereign units, will be derived from the Law of Peoples in Rawls's scheme and hence ought not to be viewed as features which parties to the contract of international justice already possess. Both internal sovereignty and external sovereignty are made to depend on the Law of Peoples. This is a commendable aspect of Rawls's argument: he makes the legitimacy of sovereignty conditional upon a state's recognition of certain principles of justice, among them respect for human rights and the commitment not to instigate war for reasons other than self-defense (Rawls 1999, 37). While we can follow Rawls's wish to impose moral constraints on traditional conceptions of state sovereignty, it is incoherent to envisage the constitutional government of a people without some form of territorial sovereignty.[2] This then creates a dilemma for Rawls's theory: either he must assume that peoples who are united by "common sympathies," and "ruled by a just constitutional government," are territorially organized as semi-sovereign units, which possess features very much like states, or he must give

---

[2] See Andrew Kuper's observation: "The difference is that in Realist theory, the shell of state sovereignty may not be pierced or removed if and when a regime acts unjustly or unreasonably – this exemplifies what I shall call 'thick statism' – whereas in Rawls's theory, the law of peoples reasonably constrains what a state may rightly do to its own people and other states; this exemplifies what I shall call 'thin statism'" (2000, 644).

up his stipulation that peoples already possess a certain form of government and simply accept a more empirical and less normative conception of peoplehood.

Peoples cannot have the following normative features which Rawls wants to ascribe to them and not be considered as organized and territorially circumscribed, self-governing modern states. Among the eight normative conditions which Rawls lists to characterize a people (ibid.), the obligation "to observe treaties and undertakings," the obligation "not to instigate war other than [in] self-defense," and "honoring human rights," while unobjectionable from a moral point of view, are hardly conceivable without a modern state apparatus with standing armies, a fully developed judicial and administrative bureaucracy, and other representative institutions. Once more, the distinction between peoples and modern states with representative governments disappears.

In his defense of Rawls, "What Self-Governing Peoples Owe to One Another: Universalism, Diversity and *The Law of Peoples*," Stephen Macedo has argued that, "The moral significance of *states or peoples* is not really so mysterious, but let us remind ourselves what a people has done in assuming the powers of self-government. They have formed a union usually understood as perpetual, and asserted a permanent control over a given territory, perhaps as the result of a violent struggle for independence" (Macedo 2004. My emphasis). Macedo clearly uses the terms peoples and states interchangeably. In doing so, he departs from the manner in which Rawls wishes to construct the steps in his theory. For Rawls, sovereign statehood must succeed peoplehood and peoples' choice of the Law of Peoples, and not precede them. Again, this would suggest that a more empirical and less normative concept of peoples needs to be stipulated, according to which they would not be viewed as already possessing a form of "just constitutional government."[3]

Rawls's third criterion of peoplehood, namely that each people should possess "a moral nature," is even harder to defend. Rawls proceeds here from a holistic understanding of peoples, each of whom is supposed to be defined by clearly delineable boundaries and by a set of clearly identifiable values and mores. In this holistic vision, peoples are viewed as carriers of a coherent moral worldview. But this holistic conception of society belongs to the infancy of the social sciences.

Missing from this vision is an appreciation of the significant internal division of human societies along the lines of class, gender, ethnicity, and religion. This holistic vision takes the aspirations of liberal-nationalist movements in their period of ascendancy in the second half of the nineteenth and early part of the twentieth century as paradigmatic, and presents these aspirations as if they were social facts. But peoples are not found; they develop through history. A crucial way in which peoples who are riven by class, gender, ethnicity, and religion develop is precisely through contestation around the terms and meaning of their common "moral nature." Excluded and marginalized groups such as workers and women in the early bourgeois republics sought to transform the moral code of the nation so as to make it more inclusive, less focused on property hierarchies and distinctions, more attuned to

[3] I cannot pursue the implications of this point for Rawls's theory construction further at this stage. I have done so elsewhere. See Benhabib 2004.

the achievements of female citizenship. Similar struggles were repeated by excluded and marginalized racial, ethnic, and religious groups. To view peoples as homogeneous entities characterized by a clearly identifiable "moral nature" and a source of "common sympathies" is not only sociologically wrong; this view is inimical to the interests of those who have been excluded from the people because they refused to accept or respect its hegemonic moral code. Rawls's vision of peoplehood slides over into nationalism. In the final analysis, his liberal-nationalist vision is more nationalist than liberal, precisely because instead of treating the hegemonic aspirations of nationalist movements to forge a people of common sympathies and a unified moral nature as ideological struggles, he confers upon them the status of sociological facts.

Suppose one defends Rawls's definition along the lines suggested by Charles Beitz: "The idea of a people is part of an ideal conception of the world. Rawls need not maintain that many (or even any) actual states fully satisfy the criteria of being a people in order to maintain that it would be desirable to move in the direction of the ideal. The appropriate question about the idea of a people is whether it represents a sufficiently desirable form of human social organization to serve as the basic constituent element of a world society, not whether it serves as a realistic proxy for any actually existing states" (2000, 680).

Beitz's defense suggests that we should judge Rawls's conception of a people ethically and not in terms of its sociological adequacy. This is not satisfactory, precisely because the sociological view entails ethical implications which significantly skew our normative vision. Rawls's understanding of peoplehood follows the tradition of liberal nationalism and nineteenth-century idealist sociology, and obscures elements of power, oppression, and ideology through which a common sense of nationality is forged.

I would contend furthermore that it is not even normatively desirable to view the Society of Peoples as a world community composed of such highly integrated, homogeneous, and homogenizing collectivities. The losers in this nationalist romance are precisely those liberal and democratic norms and values which Rawls also wants to attribute to peoples. Why? Because there is always and necessarily a contention, a disunity, a healthy disjunction between the universalizing values, norms, and principles of just constitutional government and the particularistic "common sympathies" and "moral nature" of a people. Rawls minimizes the context-transcendent aspect of the liberal-democratic values and norms which are otherwise so central to his own vision of justice and political liberalism. "We, the people," is a tension-riven formula, which seeks to contain the universalizing aspirations of rights claims and democratic sovereignty struggles within the confines of a historically situated collectivity. Such a collectivity has its "others" within and "without." Peoplehood is an aspiration; it is not a fact.

I am not seeking to make a skeptical postmodernist claim here about the instability of identity-categories. Rather, I am emphasizing that, particularly if we understand peoples to be governed by liberal-democratic institutions, there cannot be nor is it desirable that there ought to be an uncontested collective narrative of common sympathies and a unique moral nature. Collective identities are formed by strands of competing and contentious narratives in which universalizing aspirations and particularistic memories compete with one another to create temporary narrative syntheses, which are then subsequently challenged and riven by new divisions and debates. Narratives of peoplehood, and in particular of liberal-democratic peoplehood, evolve historically through such disjunctions and disputations (see Smith 2003).[4]

Rawls's view of peoples is neither ethically nor sociologically defensible and, even if we grant Rawls the legitimacy of

[4] I have presented in more detail my conception of the narrative constitution of identities in Benhabib 2002a, 6ff. I am assuming that identities are demarcated through contested narratives for two reasons: human actions and relations are formed through a double hermeneutic. We identify *what* we do through an account of *what* we do; words and deeds are equiprimordial, in the sense that almost all socially significant human actions are identified as a certain *type* of doing through the accounts that agents and others give of that doing. Second, not only are human actions and interactions constituted through a "web of narratives," but they are also constituted through the actors' *evaluative* stances toward their doings. These are second-order narratives, which entail a normative attitude toward first-order ones.

Rawls could object by claiming that the use of complicated philosophical premises and sociological theories is illicit in reasoning about justice since we have to confine ourselves to such premises as can be shared by "public culture" (Rawls 1993, 13–14, 175). I have always found this a particularly stifling aspect of Rawlsian theory, which is inimical to the enlightenment mission of much theory and philosophy. Even leaving this matter aside, however, I would argue that Rawls also relies on social science throughout his work and in *The Law of Peoples*, so that the question is not whether one utilizes assumptions and facts from sociology, history, and economics but *which kinds of facts and theories* are used. Rawls sidesteps debates between "constructivists" and "essentialists" in studies of nationalism and presents essentialism as if it were an uncontested position. See again Benhabib 2002a, 5–22, 187–189.

idealizations, these idealizations are not neutral steps toward a normative argument, but have normative consequences themselves. Alan Buchanan names a further consequence of Rawls's view: "Rawls assumes that, for purposes of a moral theory of international relations, the standard case is that of a state whose population is unified by a shared political culture, a common conception of public order – in other words, a state within which there are no conflicts over fundamental issues of justice or the good and no divisions over which groups are entitled to their own states or to special group rights" (Buchanan 2000, 717). Such a vision of "deep political unity" ignores *intrastate* conflict; it neglects the claims and grievances of groups who find neither voice nor representation for their cultures and ways of life within the confines of such a political culture. Consequently, minority-group rights or the cultural citizenship rights of peoples who are not organized as states themselves, but who are members of larger sovereign states – such as the Aborigines in Australia, First Nations in Canada, Native Americans in the USA, and the Indios in Latin America – disappear from the landscape of the Rawlsian peoples (see Benhabib 2002a on cultural group rights).

Let me return once more to Rawls's claim: "a democratic society, like any political society, is to be viewed as a *complete and closed social system*. It is complete in that it is self-sufficient and has a place for all the main purposes of human life. It is also closed . . . in that entry into it is only by birth and exit from it is only by death . . . Thus, we are not seen as joining society at the age of reason, as we might join an association, but as being born into a society where we will lead a complete life" (Rawls 1993, 41. My emphasis). In view of the preceding discussion, Rawls's point of view is more intelligible although much less defensible. Precisely because he views peoples as constituting discrete entities unified by a "common moral nature," a democratic people for Rawls comes to resemble a moral cosmos; in fact, it *is* a moral cosmos. The assumption that we enter society by birth, and that we must be viewed as "leading a complete life" within it which we exit only in death, is so wildly off the mark historically that its use by Rawls can be understood only in the light of broader presuppositions concerning peoplehood and nations.

The tension between the universalistic premises of Rawls's political liberalism and the more particularistic orientations of his Law of Peoples come fully to light around this matter. To view political society as a "complete and closed[5] social system" is incompatible with other premises of Rawlsian liberalism. Rawls understands persons to be endowed with two moral powers: a capacity to formulate and pursue an independent conception of the good; and a capacity for a sense of justice and to engage in mutual cooperative ventures with others (Rawls 1999, 82). Each of these capacities would potentially bring the individual into conflict with the vision of a democratic society as a "complete and closed system." Individuals may feel that their understanding of the good, be it for moral,

---

[5] It is unclear how Rawls intends us to understand the term "closed." Does he mean that such societies do not permit emigration or immigration? Then they would not be liberal societies but authoritarian regimes. Countries behind the Iron Curtain were "closed" in that they prohibited emigration and closely regulated internal migration. But see also Rawls 1999, 74 n. 15, on the right of emigration from "decent hierarchical" societies.

political, religious, artistic, or scientific reasons, obliges them to leave the society into which they were born and to join another society. This implies that individuals, in pursuit of their sense of the good, ought to have a right to leave their societies. Emigration must be a fundamental liberty in a Rawlsian scheme, for otherwise his conception of the person becomes incoherent. The language of a "complete and closed society" is incompatible with the liberal vision of persons and their liberties.

If it is the case that some individuals' conceptions of the good may induce them to leave their countries of birth, we also have to assume that there will be "common sympathies" and "communities of shared moral sense" which may not overlap with the boundaries of peoplehood. We speak of "a republic of letters," of "workers of the world," of "international and transnational women's groups." One of the oldest international institutions in western societies is the Catholic Church. One's sense of the moral good may or may not be coterminous with the boundaries of political community. It is most likely that individuals in liberal-democratic cultures will be creatures with multiple, and often conflicting, visions of the good; they will have overlapping attachments to partial communities; in short they will be caught in circles of overlapping and intersecting sympathy and empathy.

A crucial consequence of these reflections is that Rawls's own commitment to legitimate moral and political pluralism is jeopardized by his conception of closed societies and democratic peoplehood. While he is ready to recognize "intragroup" pluralism and to accept that there will be "decent hierarchical peoples," whose lives and values will be different than those of individuals in secular, liberal western democracies, it is odd that Rawls does not acknowledge that within western democratic societies themselves there will be many groups and individuals who bear affinity with and share the value systems of decent hierarchical peoples. Put sharply, observant Muslims and observant Jews are not "elsewhere"; they are our neighbors, citizens, and ourselves in liberal-democratic societies. Value pluralism at the *intragroup* level is parallel to value pluralism at the *intergroup* level. "The other" is not elsewhere.

The concept of a complete and closed democratic society is no more plausible than Rawls's conception of peoplehood and for much the same reason. In each case, Rawls subordinates his understanding of moral personhood to the fiction of peoplehood. There is an unresolvable tension in these formulations between the ideals of autonomous personality, even in its watered-down weak Kantian version, and that of a closed and complete society. His own understanding of the person should lead him to view societies as much more interactive, overlapping, and fluid entities, whose boundaries are permeable and porous, whose moral visions travel across borders, are assimilated into other contexts, are then reexported back into the home country, and so on.

Given both Rawls's view of peoples and the model of a "complete and closed society," it should come as no surprise that migration would not be considered an aspect of the Law of Peoples. For Rawls, migratory movements are episodic and not essential to the life of peoples; conditions of entry and exit into liberal-democratic societies are peripheral in evaluating the nature of these societies. Rather than completely abandoning immigration to non-ideal theory, that is, to political and social practices which would be "neutral" from a moral point of view, Rawls does name several conditions that would count as legitimate grounds for limiting immigration (Rawls 1999, 39).

First is a version of "the tragedy of the commons" argument. Unless a definite agent is given responsibility for maintaining an asset and bears losses for not doing so, Rawls reasons, a people's territory cannot be preserved in perpetuity for others (ibid.). This argument then leads him to the conclusion that there *must* be boundaries of some kind. Notice here that Rawls is arguing against radically open borders. But since he does not weigh the "tragedy of the commons" perspective against evidence of benefits – economic and otherwise – to be derived from open or porous borders, the reader has to accept on a commonsense basis that yes, indeed, borders of some kind are necessary. There is sufficient empirical evidence, however, that open and porous borders which enable the free movement of peoples, goods, and services across state boundaries are highly beneficial to the functioning of free-market economies. Important empirical evidence drawn from the economics of migration could offset Rawls's exclusive reliance upon the "tragedy of the commons" perspective.[6]

[6] "At a given moment, migrants are generally net contributors to the public purse: they are disproportionately of working age, and the receiving country has not had to pay for their education. A study by Britain's Home Office estimated that the foreign-born population paid about 10% more to the government than it received in expenditure. However, a magisterial study in 1997 of the economic impacts of immigration, by America's National Research Council, found that the picture changes if one looks across time instead of taking a snapshot. In that case, the NRC found, first-generation immigrants imposed an average net fiscal cost of $3,000 at present discounted value; but the second generation yielded a $80,000 fiscal gain": "A Modest Contribution," *The Economist* (November 2–8, 2002), special supplement, "A Survey of Immigration," 12–13.

Rawls's second reason for limiting immigration "is to protect a people's political culture and its constitutional principles" (ibid.). Why should Rawls assume that immigration would threaten a political culture and its constitutional principles, unless he takes it for granted that immigrants were somehow "alien and unruly elements," unlikely to be assimilated, socialized, or educated in the ways of the host country? Why does Rawls conceive of the immigrant as a threat? What historical or social-scientific basis is there for the claim that immigrants have destroyed a country's political culture rather than transforming it, that they have not defended and enriched, as well as challenged and rearticulated, constitutional principles?

Consider some contemporary cases: certainly, the predicament of the Palestinian refugees after 1948 and in the succeeding decades in Lebanon added to that country's destabilization and eventually resulted in the civil war of the 1980s. In Afghanistan, the Muslim "mujahadeen" (freedom fighters) of the Northern Alliance and the more Islamist Taliban, who had been principally organized among the Afghan refugees in Pakistan, fought together to end the Soviet invasion. The return of the Afghan refugees to their own country eventually tipped the balance in favor of the Taliban regime which then provided Al-Qaeda with a free operating ground. But these cases can hardly be considered examples of regularized migration flows or even of typical refugee and asylum resettlements. These developments are tied in with profound local dynamics, such as the already existing conflict in Lebanon among Muslim and Christian Arabs, and the radical divergence in Afghanistan among secular and religious contra-Soviet fighters. In these instances, migratory movements indeed act as catalysts to the unraveling of already existing local tensions.

Far from damaging a people's political culture and its constitution, migrants may revitalize it and deepen it. Such was the contribution of exiled liberals and socialists to the political cultures of nineteenth-century Paris and London; certainly American political culture in the late nineteenth and early twentieth century is unthinkable without the contributions of migrant Irish, Italian, Jewish, Polish, and other communities. Nor is it conceivable to think of the American university in the post-World War II period without taking into account the contributions of the many exiled European scholars. Migratory movements alone, and without crucial dislocations and tensions already at work in the receiving societies themselves, do not threaten a people's political culture and its constitutional principles. In chapter 5, I will argue that the multicultural challenge posed to political liberalism by the influx of new immigrant groups leads to a deepening and widening of the schedule of rights in liberal democracies. The "rights of others" do not threaten the project of political liberalism; quite to the contrary, they transform it toward a more inclusionary, dynamic, and deliberative democratic project.

Finally, Rawls acknowledges a "natural duty to assist burdened societies," and suggests that liberal peoples can acquit themselves of the moral obligations they owe other less fortunate societies through economic aid and assistance (Rawls 1999, 105–113). I shall discuss at more length why this natural duty of assistance needs to be distinguished carefully from a global redistributive principle. The natural duty of assistance has implications for migration rights, in that such assistance to economically poor and disadvantaged societies is expected to reduce the pressure of migratory movements on richer societies. In a world of great economic disparities, in which the pull of a higher standard of living in wealthier countries is an undeniable cause of migrations, such assistance could certainly help ease pressure in some regions of the world for certain periods of time (see *The Economist*, November 2–8, 2002, special supplement, "A Survey of Immigration"). Rawls's perspective would thus justify that nations that give foreign aid to those countries or regions of the world from which the emigrants come could impose a harsh regime of migration, so as to minimize entry into their societies. Moral balancing acts between duties of assistance to others and the legitimate self-interest of states are endemic to migration debates and policies; they are indeed part of the arsenal of realist politics in this domain. As commonsensical as such balancing acts appear, however, they need to be constrained by careful distinctions between refugees and asylum seekers toward whom states have not only moral but also legal obligations, and the moral claims of migrants. These distinctions, which were so crucial to the cosmopolitan considerations of Kant and Arendt, find no place in Rawls's scheme. I do not believe that this omission is a matter of oversight alone. I rather think that it is a consequence of Rawls's ideal theory of peoples in the world community.

Rawls's realist utopia aims at a radical solution to the world's migratory movements. In a society of liberal and decent peoples, there would be no persecution of religious and ethnic minorities, no political oppression, no population pressures, and no inequality between men and women, and economic inequalities would diminish. Thus, "The problem of immigration is not, then, simply left aside, but is eliminated as a serious problem in a realistic utopia" (Rawls 1999, 39). In Rawls's ideal utopia, peoples become windowless monads who have no interest in mixing, mingling, and interacting with others. This is certainly a vision of an ordered world but it is also the vision of a static, dull world of self-satisfied peoples, who are indifferent not only to each other's plight but to each other's charms as well.

In conclusion, then: the Rawlsian Law of Peoples does not continue upon the terrain charted by Kant's doctrine of cosmopolitan right in that Rawls does not consider individuals to be the moral and political agents of a world society, but rather chooses peoples to be the principal actors in this arena. Notwithstanding disclaimers to the contrary, Rawls cannot distinguish analytically between peoples and states, with the consequence that cosmopolitan right is sacrificed in the altar of states' security and self-interest. Rawls is admirably clear on where he departs from views of cosmopolitan justice. "Some think," he writes, "that any liberal Law of Peoples . . . should begin by first taking up the question of liberal cosmopolitan or global justice for all persons. They argue that in such a view all persons are considered to be reasonable and rational and to possess what I have called 'the two moral powers' . . . Following the kind of reasoning familiar in the original position for the domestic case, the persons would then adopt a first principle that all persons have equal basic rights and liberties. Proceeding this way would straightaway ground human rights in a political (moral) conception of liberal cosmopolitan justice" (ibid., 82).

Rawls believes that it is implausible to proceed in this way, for this procedure would impose a metaphysical or comprehensive view of liberalism upon all peoples. He rejects this philosophically, but he also seems concerned that such a position would necessarily lead to an expansionist, intolerant, and possibly even belligerent foreign policy on the part of liberal peoples (ibid., 82–83).

In the next chapter I will formulate a discourse-theoretic grounding of rights discourse and I will try to show that one need not appeal to controversial metaphysical premises to do so. Furthermore, to endorse cosmopolitan right does not mean imposing a *specific schedule of rights* upon all peoples. The *principle of rights* permits considerable democratic variation, although not as much as Rawls would like to allow.

I have argued that Rawls's commitment to legitimate moral and political pluralism is compromised by his vision of democratic peoples as living in closed societies. Precisely a more radical pluralism would lead to the acknowledgment of the multiple and dynamic ties, interactions, and crisscrossings of peoples. As opposed to the vision of a "closed" society into which individuals are born and which they leave only in death, I shall proceed from the assumption that liberal peoples have "fairly open borders"; that they not only permit a fundamental right to *emigrate*, but that they coexist within a system of mutual obligations and privileges, an essential component of which is the privilege to *immigrate*, that is, to enter another people's territory and become a member of its society peacefully. Peoples are radically and not merely episodically interdependent. Nation-states develop in history as units of a system of states. They emerge out of the ruins of old multinational

93

empires. Large numbers of nation-states emerged in Europe and the Middle East after the collapse of the Austro-Hungarian, the Russian, and the Ottoman empires at the end of World War I. The decolonization struggles against the British, French, Portuguese, and Dutch empires in the aftermath of World War II resulted in new states being born in Asia, Africa, and elsewhere. Beginning in the nineteenth century, Latin American nations struggled against the Spanish empire. I view peoples and states as actors developing in the context of a world society. The nation-state, which combines territorial sovereignty with aspirations to cultural homogeneity and democratic constitutional government, is a unique product of world society as it undergoes political modernization.

Toward a radicalized Rawlsianism

Moral cosmopolitanism

It should come as no surprise that, for many students of Rawls, his views on cosmopolitan justice have proven a source of disappointment. Radicalizing Rawls's intentions against Rawls himself, Joseph Carens has drawn completely different conclusions from Rawlsian premises. In an early article, Carens used the device of the Rawlsian "veil of ignorance," against the intentions of Rawls himself, to think through principles of justice from the standpoint of the refugee, the immigrant, and the asylum seeker (Carens 1995). Are the borders within which we happen to be born, and the documents to which we are entitled, any less arbitrary from a moral point of view than other characteristics such as skin color, gender, and genetic make-up with which we are endowed? Carens's answer is "no." From a moral point of view, the borders which circumscribe our birth and the papers to which we are entitled are arbitrary, since their distribution among individuals does not follow any clear criteria of moral achievement and moral compensation. Citizenship status and privileges, which are simply based upon territorially defined birthright, are no less arbitrary than one's skin color and other genetic endowments. Therefore, claims Carens, liberal democracies should practice policies which are as compatible as possible with the vision of a world without borders.[7]

---

[7] Cosmopolitan citizenship, as advocated by Martha Nussbaum, entails not so much a political practice as a moral attitude of not placing the affairs and concerns of one's immediate community ahead of those others who may be strangers to us, residing in faraway worlds. In Nussbaum's version, cosmopolitanism is a universalist ethic that denies the claims upon us of what are referred to in moral theory as "special obligations" (Nussbaum 1996, 1997). These are obligations that emerge out of our situatedness in concrete human communities of descent or sympathy, genealogy or affiliation. Nussbaum denies that "patriotism," or a privileged commitment to a specific territorially bounded national community, constitutes such a special obligation. Patriotism does not trump "the love of humanity," and should not lead us to ignore the needs of others with whom we share neither culture nor descent, neither genealogy nor history (Nussbaum 1996, 12–17). I agree with Martha Nussbaum that a cosmopolitical attitude lies at the core of moral universalism, and must oblige the moral agent to mediate the demands of the universal with the draw of the particular (see Benhabib 1992). It is less clear what *political*, as opposed to *moral*, practices such a cosmopolitan moral attitude would entail, and which institutions, if any, would correspond to this mindset.

Liberal cosmopolitanism

In recognition of the difficulties of translating universal moral obligations into viable political forms at the global level, Thomas Pogge has distinguished between "moral cosmopolitanism," which asserts that "every human being has a global stature as an ultimate unit of moral concern" (1992, 49), and "legal cosmopolitanism." Legal cosmopolitanism is committed, in Pogge's words, "to a concrete political ideal of a global order under which all persons have equivalent legal rights and duties, that is, are fellow citizens of a universal republic" (ibid.). Pogge wants to defend a set of institutionalized global ground rules which, while falling short of a world state, will nonetheless move the global status quo toward a more cosmopolitan world order in the legal sense.

Pogge's formulations remind us of a difficulty which Kant had also confronted, namely, whether moral cosmopolitanism would inevitably result in a "universal monarchy," i.e., a world government. Kant argued that such a world government would be a "soulless despotism" (Kant [1795] 1923, 453; [1795] 1957, 112). While rejecting the idea of a world state, Kant embraced the idea of a society of peoples, each of whom was informed by a set of similar republican principles, which, nonetheless, permitted some variation. Is legal cosmopolitanism, then, compatible with republican or democratic freedom? What variation in legal institutions and the schedule of human rights is permissible within a legal cosmopolitan framework?

A clear implication of any moral and legal cosmopolitan position is that existing disparities in the living standards and life expectations of the world's peoples ought to be subject to critique and reform. As was the case for Kant, for Pogge and Beitz too it is *individuals* who are the units of moral and legal rights in a world society and not *peoples*. Peoples' interactions are continuous and not episodic; their lives and livelihood are radically, and not only intermittently, interdependent, as they were in the Rawlsian model of peoples. While neither Pogge (1992, 60–61) nor Beitz[8] directly addresses matters of immigration, their positions have clear implications for migration rights and just membership.

The duty of assistance versus global distributive justice

For Rawls, "Well-ordered people have a *duty* to assist burdened societies" (Rawls 1999, 106).[9] Yet it is not the case "that the only way, or the best way, to carry out this duty of

[8] Commenting on Henry Sidgwick's plea for restricting immigration in order to maintain a society's internal cohesion, Beitz points out that, "under contemporary conditions, it seems unlikely that the value derived by their citizens from the cohesion and order of relatively well-endowed societies is greater than the value that could be gained by others from the redistribution of labor (or wealth) that would be brought about by adherence to cosmopolitan policies" (Beitz [1979] 1999, 209). Liberal cosmopolitans see migratory flows as aspects of global redistribution through which the poor of the earth claim a share of the wealth of richer countries by seeking access to them.

[9] The sources of this "duty" are left unclear by Rawls. While the duty to assist others in need is included in most systems of individual morality, whether Kantian, rule-utilitarian, or intuitionist, it is unclear what the sources of such obligations among collectivities would be. One possible answer is that the Society of Peoples must be viewed as a system of

assistance is by following a principle of global distributive justice to regulate economic and social inequalities among peoples" (ibid.). To many this claim has seemed inconsistent at
best and hypocritical at worst. Thomas Pogge observes with
sarcasm: "As it is, the moral debate is largely focused on the
question to what extent affluent societies and persons have obligations to help others worse off than themselves. Some deny
all such obligations, others claim them to be quite demanding. Both sides easily take for granted that it is as potential
helpers that we are morally related to the starving abroad. This
is true, of course. *But the debate ignores that we are also and
much more significantly related to them as supporters of, and
beneficiaries from, a global institutional order that substantially
contributes to their destitution*" (Pogge 2002, 50. My emphasis).
A similar criticism was expressed by Charles Beitz in *Political Theory and International Relations:* "International interdependence involves a complex and substantial pattern of social
interaction, which produces benefits and burdens that would
not exist if national economies were autarkic. In view of these
considerations, Rawls's passing concern for the law of nations
seems to miss the point of international justice altogether. In
an interdependent world, confining principles of justice to

cooperation in which each people has a duty to improve the conditions
of all, such that some form of equality among them may be attained. If
this is Rawls's reasoning (cf. Rawls 1999, 18–19), then liberal
cosmopolitans such as Beitz and Pogge are justified in asking why a
system of cooperation may not be subjected to even more demanding
criteria of equality among the cooperating parties. To reiterate a phrase
made famous by Rawls in *A Theory of Justice*, why should people take "an
interest in one another's interests" ([1971] 1972, 13)?

domestic societies has the effect of taxing poor nations so that others may benefit from living in 'just' regimes" ([1979]1999, 149–150).

This disagreement about the scope and content of principles of distributive justice on a global scale involves methodological as well as empirical divergences among Rawls and his more radical followers. Rawls, while not denying that the international system is one of interdependencies, clearly views this fact to be of secondary importance in determining a country's wealth or poverty. The causes of the wealth of nations are endogenous and not exogenous. A country's wealth is determined by "its political culture," and by religious, philosophical, and moral traditions that support its basic structure, as well as by the moral qualities of its people, such as their industriousness and cooperative talents (Rawls 1999, 109). There is remarkably little social-scientific evidence which Rawls adduces to support this assertion.[10] These claims rest less on empirical evidence and more on Rawls's methodological takeoff point that considers liberal peoples as living in well-ordered societies, whose good fortune is a consequence of their own institutions and moral nature. In this remarkably Victorian account of the wealth of nations, the plunder of Africa by all western societies is not mentioned even once; the

---

[10] Rawls cites David Landes, *The Wealth and Poverty of Nations* (1998); Amartya Sen, *Poverty and Famine* (1981); and Jean Drèze and Sen, *Hunger and Public Action* (1989). But Sen's perspective on these matters is much more globalist and structural, and less culturalist and nation-state-centered than Landes's. Rawls slides over these differences.

global character of the African slave trade and its contribution to the accumulation of capitalist wealth in the United States and the Caribbean basin are barely recalled; the colonization of the Americas disappears from view; and it is as if the British never dominated India and exploited its riches. These historical omissions are of such magnitude in a work on the Law of Peoples that we have to ask why Rawls has imposed blinders which affect his sight of international justice so drastically.

My purpose is not to rehash well-known debates in the social sciences about the origins of capitalism in the West – the so-called good fortune of liberal peoples – and the interdependence of capitalism and imperialism. I take it that it would be historically grossly inadequate to consider the development of capitalism without also taking into account the history of western imperialism (Schama 1987; Hobsbawm 1975, 1987; Meuschel 1981; Genovese [1965] 1990; Genovese-Fox and Genovese 1983). It is also not necessary to render quick judgments on these complex world-historical processes: whether early capitalist accumulation in the West could have been conceivable without colonial expansion is doubtful, but it is equally clear, as Max Weber ([1930] 1992) has instructed us, that the moral-cultural and value transformations leading to the formation of the Protestant ethic in the West had indigenous sources. These sources lie in the intellectual and moral dynamic of the scientific and Protestant revolutions, which, although they eventually attained worldwide significance, formed a unique configuration in the West alone.[11] The

[11] The numbers system originated in India, the ancient Chinese knew a great deal about scientific and experimental methods, and, without the efforts of Arab and Jewish philosophers in the Middle Ages to preserve

wealth of nations needs to be examined in light of the history of the world economy: the methodological distortions caused by assumptions of cultural autarky need to be discarded. I join Beitz when he writes that "It is easier to demonstrate that a pattern of global interdependence exists, and that it yields substantial aggregate benefits, than to say with certainty how these benefits are distributed under existing institutions and practices or what burdens these institutions and practices impose on participants in the world economy" (Beitz [1979] 1999, 145).

Does the fact of global interdependence suggest that the world economic system is a "system of cooperation"? A system of cooperation would suggest that the rules distributing obligations as well as benefits would be clearly identifiable and known, or in principle knowable,[12] to the participants. Since he denies that the world economy can be understood along these lines, Rawls maintains that principles of distributive justice cannot be applied to this domain. Whereas in a

the thought and work of Greek philosophers, the Renaissance in the West could not have occurred. The debt of cultures to one another is even more extensive than economic history alone would suggest.

[12] I introduce this caveat for the following reason: although I may not know how the car insurance or the social security system works, how insurance premiums are set and social security benefits disbursed, in principle, I could find out if I chose to. A system of cooperation, as opposed to a system of "unintended consequences," is based on knowable rules and regulations. Social and economic life, however, is governed by both schemes: systems of cooperation as well as the logic of unintended consequences. The economic market is a social sphere which combines both features. Some would even argue that it can function as a system of cooperation precisely because it is based on the logic of unintended consequences.

system of cooperation there would be clear rules or patterns for distributing benefits and obligations, the world economy can hardly be the object of such clear and transparent judgments. Thus global distributive-justice principles, despite their considerable appeal, do not have "a defined goal, aim, or cut-off point" (Rawls 1999, 106). I think that Rawls is only partially right in this objection. The world economy, while not being a pure system of cooperation, incorporates organizations such as the World Trade Organization and the International Monetary Fund, which have very clear rules of cooperation, as well as encompassing the vast myriad of patterns and trends generated by the unintended consequences of individual actors.

The world economy, or for that matter any economic system, possesses features of cooperation as well as the logic of unintended consequences. Think for example of the stock market: while there are clearly defined rules of cooperation – at least in principle – as to how stocks can be bought and sold, as to how their values are rated, and the like, at the end of the day what makes the stock market work is precisely "the logic of unintended consequences." Once these rules of cooperation are established, no one can predict and in principle ought not to be able to predict what results the market produces. Insider trading is regulated because it skews the logic of unintended consequences by destroying the fairness of the rules of cooperation. Unlike free-marketers, I have no faith that the logic of unintended consequences is always rational or just. Obviously, governments and other regulatory agencies interfere precisely to rectify dysfunctionalities resulting from the play of market forces. It is hardly conceivable, for example, that a government would permit the social security fund to go bankrupt as a result of the vagaries of the market place, although free-market ideologues and privatization prophets have been known to advocate liquefying such assets. If we concede to Rawls that the world economy is not a pure system of cooperation, but a mixed domain showing features of cooperation and competition, organization and the logic of unintended consequences, what follows for the global redistributive position?

The world economy, while falling short of being a system of cooperation, is one of significant interdependences with non-negligible distributive consequences for the players involved. Within this system, there are international bodies and organizations which have regulatory functions such as the World Trade Organization, the International Monetary Fund, the Agency for International Development and treaty associations such as the General Agreement on Tariffs and Trade and North American Free Trade Agreement. Increasingly, these organizations are moving toward a model of global cooperation, which would control and ameliorate the havoc that the logic of unintended consequences can cause. Thus global-justice theorists are right in demanding, contra Rawls, that these international bodies ought to be rendered increasingly accountable in their actions and transparent in their decision-making to their constituencies. Even if the world economy is not a system of cooperation, precisely because it reveals significant patterns of interdependence, as well as being influenced by quasi-governing bodies, there is a great deal of room for reform here which would go well beyond the natural duty of assistance to burdened peoples.

The world community, I want to suggest, should be viewed as a global civil society, in which peoples organized as states are major players, but by no means the only players. A cosmopolitan perspective takes as its starting point the Kantian view that, "if the actions of one can affect the actions of another," then we have an obligation to regulate our actions under a common law of freedom which respects our equality as moral agents. The consequences of our actions generate moral obligations; once we become aware of how in fact they influence the well-being and freedom of others, we must assume responsibility for the unintended and invisible consequences of our individual and collective doings. We are constantly discovering such interdependencies and becoming aware that what we eat, drink, smoke, and consume as energy in our homes and our cars have a substantial impact upon the lives of others to whom we may not be even remotely related. There is a dialectic here between the growth of social knowledge and the spread of moral responsibility. In Kantian language, if the will of one can limit the will of another in the external domain of actions, then we become intertwined in the moral net of responsibilities and obligations. Such is the situation with the world economy: while very clear judgments about the specific effects of this or that policy upon others' lives and well-being may not always be at hand, we are constantly being challenged in understanding the moral implications of our actions by discovering unintended consequences as well as by becoming aware of the regulatory and interventionist measures of world governing bodies. Such knowledge creates moral responsibility. It is no longer morally permissible for car drivers and industries in Chicago, for example, to ignore that their actions are causing acid rain in Canada; nor should it be possible for those living in the United States to ignore that the agricultural abundance of California is owed, in large measure even if not wholly, to the sweat, blood, and toil of illegal Mexican workers, whose cheap seasonal labor has made possible the harvest of abundance we reap.

The conclusion that Beitz and Pogge draw from similar analyses is that a global redistributive principle must be applicable to the world economic system. Beitz writes that "In particular, if the difference principle ('social and economic inequalities are to be arranged so that they are . . . to the greatest benefit of the least advantaged') would be chosen in the domestic original position, it would be chosen in the global original position as well" ([1979] 1999, 151). Pogge concurs (2002, 42).

The debate as to whether a global redistributive principle ought to be formulated as some version of a Rawlsian difference principle or in some version of Pogge's global egalitarian principle is not one that I wish to pursue further. I agree with Beitz's and Pogge's liberal cosmopolitan vision that in a world of radical, and not merely accidental and transitory, interdependencies among peoples, our distributive obligations go well beyond the natural duty of assistance. However, I am made uncomfortable by the imposition of a global redistributive principle to create economic justice among peoples, unless and until the compatibility of such a principle with democratic self-governance is examined. I will present three objections to global redistributionism and I will distinguish the latter from the cosmopolitan federalist perspective, which I wish to defend and which has redistributionist implications as well. Let me call the first objection epistemic; the second, hermeneutic; and the third democratic.

The epistemic objection

Even if the world economy is best understood as a system of significantly patterned interdependencies and causal interconnections, generalized judgments about aggregate responsibilities are difficult to make. While we can calculate how the carbon-monoxide-emission levels of advanced industrial countries are damaging the world's atmosphere, it is much more difficult – even if not impossible – to calculate how consumption patterns of meat in the USA may or may not be affecting the Mexican economy or whether the economic downturn in Germany is causing unemployment in Greece, and what should be done about these.

With reference to the economic causes of migration, for example, Hania Zlotnik writes: "Given that economic considerations are at the root of most international migration, the latter is significantly influenced by developments in the world economy ... The promotion of freer trade either within trading blocs or at a more general level is deemed to have important consequences for international migration ... However, since the process of development itself is recognized to set in motion forces that promote migration, it is not evident whether the successful participation of developing countries in the world economy and the trading system will *enhance or reduce* the potential for international migration" (Zlotnik 2001, 228. My emphasis).

In the absence of more precise judgments about global economic causalities, to extend the difference principle, with its radically redistributive agenda, to the world economy is a fallacy of misplaced concreteness. When we are dealing with as complex a moral and epistemic object as the world economic system, setting general global goals, upon which democratic consensus can be generated, is more desirable. We ought to treat the difference principle, which proceeds from a rather controversial aggregation of individual assets in the first place, as a guideline and a normative goal rather than as a specific policy for reducing inequalities. Reducing world hunger, infant mortality, illiteracy, death from malnutrition and lack of adequate sanitation, eradication of diseases, and the like are goals upon which there is growing consensus in the world community. Redistribution of wealth and assets, by way of development aid, is certainly one of the important ways in which such goals can be attained, but it is not the only way; others would include sustainable growth projects; helping indigenous industries and economies to develop through small loans; liberalizing and democratizing the governance of institutions such as the World Bank and International Monetary Fund; making criteria for the award of loans and grants from world-lending institutions more transparent and democratic; debt amnesty for struggling third-world economies; and controlling and penalizing speculations in financial markets which endanger weak economies. I do not share the theoretical certainty behind the difference principle: it is a *criterion* of judgment, not a blueprint for policy. It was intended by Rawls as a theoretical criterion to improve upon Pareto-optimality in measuring the justice of economic institutions; it ought not to be viewed as a map for rearranging institutions.

The hermeneutic objection

In *Situating the Self: Gender, Community and Postmodernism in Contemporary Ethics*, I argued that the Rawlsian original position could not accommodate adequate moral individuation (Benhabib 1992, 164–170). Behind the Rawlsian veil of ignorance, I maintained, the other as distinct from the self would disappear, because all the significant criteria for individuating selves would be hidden behind the veil. Under this construction, we would not be reversing moral perspectives and reasoning from the standpoint of the other, for the other and the self would become identical and each reasoning for himself alone could reason for all others.

A similar difficulty attaches to the difference principle. Since I consider this difficulty quite important, I see no plausible reason to extend the difference principle to the global arena. Any application of the difference principle across borders presupposes that we share clear and non-controversial judgments about who is to count as "the least advantaged" member of society. I do not believe that we possess such clear criteria, for this is not an econometric judgment alone, but a political-economic one. Certainly, plenty of empirical information is available about income distribution, life expectancy, levels of education, and the like in many societies and in the world at large. Yet there is very little consensus about which of these criteria ought to be taken as forming the baseline against which to measure the status of being "least advantaged." Amartya Sen has convincingly argued against the fetishization of econometric data and has maintained that, as opposed to global economic comparisons based on per capita GNP, which tell very little about the actual life conditions of the populations assessed, "quality of life" measurements would require much more differentiated assessments of "human capacities" (Sen 1984, 1999).

The global application of the difference principle, by contrast, implies that there is much more convergence and consensus around controversial political and economic judgments than there is and will ever be in a world community. I therefore conclude, as I did in the consideration of the epistemic principle, that setting global guidelines, norms, and standards that permit local interpretation is far more desirable than assuming that a globally shared standard for measuring well-being exists.[13]

---

[13] In conversation Nancy Fraser raised the following objection. Wouldn't there be similiar epistemic and hermeneutic divergences *within* states as well and wouldn't this imply that redistributive measures within the polity are themselves illegitimate? I think that there are vast epistemic and hermeneutic differences of opinion on these matters in all democratic societies. As opposed to the global context, however, such democratic societies exhibit several features: (a) a public sphere of opinion and exchange in which free debate about who "the least advantaged" among the population are can be carried out; (b) a common framework of governance which creates clear lines of accountability, such that changes in redistributive policy can be measured and articulated; (c) the possibility, as well as the necessity, of forging temporary points of democratic convergence on reconciling differing conceptions of equality.

Bodies such as the IMF, the World Bank, and the AID are increasingly assuming functions of governance without being subject to

The democratic objection

The crucial challenge that globalists face is that of reconciling democratic politics with global egalitarian aspirations. Since a global redistributive principle assumes a high degree of epistemic and hermeneutic convergence, we can expect that it will need to be administered by a world government or by some world authority with significant powers of coercion and enforcement. Beitz and Pogge are sensitive to this objection and defend themselves against visions of world government.[14] Beitz distinguishes *the moral responsibilities* of redistributive justice from the *institutions* of global justice. Yet if the consequences of the former entail significant losses for the latter, if the tradeoff is between justice and democracy, then we must pause and reconsider our alternatives. Given existing levels of low cooperation around the world economy, it is unlikely that a global redistributive principle in the form of a difference principle can ever gain consensus. But where, then, does this leave us?

Socioeconomic justice and criteria by which to measure it cannot be identified independently of practices of

these democratic constraints. But they ought to be. My argument is not anti-redistributionist at all; it is an attempt to reconcile democratic decision-making with redistributive policies.

14 Cf. Beitz who writes: "It is a mistake to identify too closely the scope of the principles and the scope of the institutions necessary to implement them, for a variety of configurations and institutions can be imagined (for example, a coordinated set of regional institutions) that would implement the principle" ([1979] 1999, 157). See also Pogge, who advocates "nested territorial units," in a "multi-layered scheme" (Pogge 1992, 68).

democratic freedom and self-determination. The hermeneutic puzzles raised by the difference principle can be dealt with,
though never completely resolved, only in a democratic context. Democratic peoples themselves must form judgments
about economic priorities and enlighten themselves about how
these priorities bear on matters of social and economic justice
in their societies. Precisely because there is no certainty on these
matters even among experts, judgments as to who constitutes
the "worst off" in a society or in the world at large require complex democratic processes of opinion and will-formation. As
theorists we can intervene in this process through our projects,
proposals, criticisms, and suggestions, but we must not pre-
empt democratic processes by all-too-hasty formulations of
redistributive schemes.

Pogge may object and claim that such democratic processes are unlikely to yield more global justice than they do
now: they will merely leave an extremely unjust and inegalitar-
ian world pretty much as it is. Certainly democratic selfishness
is a risk we must be willing to countenance. Yet the stark jux-
taposition of global justice and democratic selfishness is itself
unsatisfactory because it distorts the complex interdependence
of justice and democracy.

First, socioeconomic equality is itself a precondition
for the effective exercise of democratic citizenship rights. The
equal value of liberty for citizens can be realized only if they
also have access to and enjoy a bundle of rights and entitlements which are necessary for them to lead lives of human
dignity and autonomy. In democratic societies, access to and
enjoyment of rights and entitlements are crucial aspects of the
meaning of citizenship (see further ch. 4). So the disagreement

between myself and the globalists is not about whether socio-economic equality is necessary to democratic citizens' equality; it clearly is. Rather, we disagree about the acceptable *margin of democratic divergence* in the interpretation and concretization of socioeconomic rights and entitlements.

I concur with Ian Shapiro when he writes: "Allowing an equal say in a decision to people with greatly differing stakes in the outcome generates pathologies similar to those involving large differences in capacities for exit . . . Those whose basic interests are at stake in a particular decision have a stronger claim to inclusion in the demos than those for whom this is not so" (Shapiro 1999, 235). Shapiro's principle of "affected interests" is quite similar to the principle of discourse ethics which likewise demands that all those whose interests are affected by a policy, a norm, and their consequences have a say in their articulation as equals in a practical discourse. And the circle of those whose interests are affected will vary locally as well as globally.

Second, within the world community viewed as a global civil society, there are multiple levels of organization, association, and networks of interdependence, each of which can permit a variety of principles of organization. Multilayered governance in a world community can ameliorate stark oppositions between global aspirations and local self-determination. Thus the democratic principles of transparency and accountability need to be extended to organizations such as the WTO, IMF, and AID, while reforming international institutions such as the UN Security Council to be more inclusive of the voices of nations other than the five with permanent seats has become crucial in this juncture. While democratizing these bodies alone may not be sufficient to ameliorate global inequality, other forms of cooperation among regional economies and regional trade and growth associations can also mediate between transnational standards and local conditions. If we view the world economy as constituted by multiple levels and layers of governance, cooperation, and coordination, the question becomes one of mediating among these varied levels so as to create more convergence on some commonly agreed-upon standards for the eradication of poverty, but through locally, nationally, or regionally interpreted, instituted, and organized initiatives. Schemes for sustainable economic development, through which each country's specific conditions and capacities are considered and economic projects tailored according to local conditions, would be pertinent examples in this domain.

I will call such processes of interaction among actors in complex, multilayered contexts of governance forms of *democratic iteration.* Democratic iterations are moral and political dialogues in which global principles and norms are reappropriated and reiterated by constituencies of all sizes, in a series of interlocking conversations and interactions. Concerns for global justice can thereby become guiding principles of action for democratic peoples themselves. Although such processes may be messy and unpredictable and may yield less than ideal results, they are preferable to global redistributive principles, which, though they may be based on the best and purest of intentions, have to rely on coercive enforcement agencies whose democratic credentials are questionable. "Ought" implies "can." The alternatives we face in thinking about international distribution are not between pure global justice on the one hand and democratic governance on the other, but, rather, "democratic justice" (see Shapiro 1999), leading through a series of interlocking, overlapping, and intersecting institutional mechanisms to global justice. This is also the vision of federated cosmopolitanism which I will discuss further in chapter 5.

Questioning cosmopolitanism: the decline-of-citizenship theorists

Certainly the best-known objections to the globalist vision have been voiced by a group of thinkers at times referred to as communitarians, at others as civic republicans, and even as liberal nationalists. Whether they believe it is their society's cultural cohesion or the integrity of its political institutions that is threatened by mass migrations and the growing porousness of borders, communitarians, civic republicans, and liberal nationalists are concerned that cosmopolitans are not sufficiently sensitive to the *special attachments* which individuals have to their homes and countries. The following statement by Michael Walzer captures the concerns of a range of thinkers who oppose the cosmopolitan alternative:

> To tear down the walls of the state is not, as Sidgwick worriedly suggested, to create a world without walls, but rather to create a thousand petty fortresses. The fortresses, too, can be torn down: all that is necessary is a global state sufficiently powerful to overwhelm the local communities. Then the result would be the world of the political economist, as Sidgwick described it (or of global capitalism, I might add) – *a world of deracinated men and women.* (Walzer 1983, 39)

While morally and legally I subscribe to the cosmopolitan alternative, politically I believe that decline-of-citizenship theorists raise important concerns about the need for democratic self-governance and the legitimacy of boundaries. Nevertheless, if liberal cosmopolitans place global justice ahead of democratic process, decline-of-citizenship theorists err by conflating the boundaries of the *political community* with those of the *ethical one.* They are also guilty of neglecting political institutions while focusing excessively on cultural identities.

Decline-of-citizenship theorists show more sensitivity toward the democratic paradox, which I have outlined in chapter 1. They respect the collective will of self-governing communities in wanting to protect and define boundaries. In doing so, however, they overemphasize the degree of internal cohesion within the political community and they seek to steer clear of "rights talks." Yet respect for universalistic rights principles and collective self-determination claims are the two poles of legitimacy for democratic polities. They must be renegotiated, reappropriated, and rearticulated in creative public political dialogues, including but not exclusively restricted to ones about immigration.

Migration and the decline of citizenship

The decline-of-citizenship school includes communitarians, civic republicans, and liberal nationalists as well as social democrats (Sandel 1996; Jacobson 1997; Walzer 1983 and 2001; Offe 1998; Streeck 1998; Hobsbawm 1996). These thinkers consider the waning of the nation-state, whether under the impact of economic globalization, the rise of international human rights norms, or the spread of attitudes of cosmopolitical detachment, as resulting in the devaluation of citizenship as institution and practice.[15] Citizenship entails membership in a bounded community; the right to the determination of the boundaries as well as identity of this community are fundamental to democracy; therefore, they argue, economic and political globalization threaten to undermine citizenship. While immigration is not precluded by these theorists, they tend to favor the incorporation only of those foreigners who "are like us," and who can become "model citizens" (Honig 2001).

Surely, the decline-of-citizenship school is correct in raising concerns about the transformation of citizenship in contemporary democracies, yet they are wrong in tracing the causes of these transformations back to liberalized practices of membership and to the increased worldwide mobility of peoples. The decline of citizenship, if measured in terms of political participation rates or even in terms of civic participation at large, as a significant body of recent scholarship has recently demonstrated, has domestic as well as global causes (see Putnam 2001, 2003). Immigration and porous borders,

---

[15] For an important analysis and critique of the sociological as well as normative assumptions of these theories, see Veit Bader who writes: "The core of the *sociological* arguments lies in the construction of a stylized normativity of the modern nation-state in which the borders of the state coincide with the 'functional completeness' of the economy and 'practical self-understanding of the nation as a community of values.' ... 'Economic globalization or internationalization' and institutional internationalization (e.g. the EU) inevitably lead to a 'decoupling of the borders of economy, society and the state'" (Bader forthcoming; quoting from Streeck 1998). Bader justifiably points out that there is little evidence for this historical idealization.

rather than being causes of the decline of citizenship, are themselves caused by the same maelstroms which are undermining national political institutions: namely, the globalization of capital, financial, and labor markets (although people are never as mobile as money and assets); lack of control over the movements of stocks and bonds; emergence of catchall and ideologically non-differentiated mass parties; the rise of mass media politics and the eclipse of local votes and campaigns. This general malaise can hardly be blamed on migrants, refugees, and asylees. Nor is the perception that migrants are passive and apolitical agents, who are simply swept around by global market forces, correct. There are new modalities of political agency, sprouting amidst the institutions of the unbundling or disaggregation of citizenship rights, even on the part of those who do not possess full membership.[16] These new modalities are changing the meaning of political citizenship and activism. The "decline of citizenship" theorists ignore the emergence of these new actors and new modes of political activism.[17] (See ch. 5 below.)

Michael Walzer is among the few contemporary theorists who have addressed the significance of questions of membership for theories of justice as well as for theories of democracy. His position is built around one aspect of the paradox of democratic legitimacy, which I identify as being

---

[16] For an important analysis of political activism among Europe's guest worker communities in the Netherlands, see Tillie and Slijper forthcoming.

[17] See the important collection of essays, *Immigration and Citizenship in the Twenty-First Century*, edited by Noah Pickus (1998), and in particular the contributions of Juan Perea (1998) and Michael Jones-Correa (1998).

caused by the dual allegiance to human rights norms and to collective self-determination. Walzer is skeptical, or maybe better still, agnostic about universal human rights claims. He privileges the will of the political sovereign while seeking to leaven the possible injustices and inequities which may result from such acts and policies by considerations of fairness and compassion, sensitive contextual reasoning and moral openness. I want to argue that, as attractive as it may seem, this strategy is inadequate and that dilemmas of political membership in liberal democracies go to the heart of the self-definition, as well as self-constitution, of these polities precisely because, as liberal democracies, they are built on the constitutive tension between human rights and political sovereignty claims.

Even when it is admitted that immigrants can be "good citizens," advocates of community control maintain that defining the quality and quantity of movements across borders should remain a *sovereign privilege* of the democratic people alone. Thus for Walzer in *Spheres of Justice*, polities ought to be free to define conditions of *first entry*, be it for immigrants or for refugees and asylees, as they see fit within the confines of their international obligations. "[A]ctually to take in large numbers of refugees is often morally necessary; but the right to restrain the flow remains a feature of communal self-determination. The principle of mutual aid can only modify and not transform *admissions policies rooted in a particular community's understanding of itself*" (Walzer 1983, 51. My emphasis). Should they choose to meet their responsibilities to help refugees and asylees, not through liberal entry policies but through foreign economic and development aid, thereby encouraging refugees to return to their homes or not to leave at all, they should be able to do so. For example, faced with large numbers of refugees fleeing Haiti in the 1990s, the Clinton administration intervened to enable the reinstallation of the (since deposed) regime of Jean-Bertrand Aristide thus securing the refugees' return. From Michael Walzer's point of view, this is a perfectly acceptable way of satisfying one's moral obligations. Walzer also argues that, once individuals have been admitted into a country, they cannot remain foreigners forever and must be naturalized. Yet the basis for this claim is unclear; there certainly is no such thing as a human right to membership in Walzer's view; why existing polities should feel an obligation to naturalize foreigners is left unexplained.

What exactly would be "admissions policies rooted in a particular community's understanding of itself"? Couldn't this formula lead to compromising the moral and legal commitments of nations to the rights of refugees and asylees on the grounds that admitting them would be "diluting or impairing communal and cultural self-understandings"? "The distinctiveness of cultures and groups," writes Walzer, "depends upon closure and, without it, cannot be conceived as a stable feature of human life. If this distinctiveness is a value, as most people (though some of them are global pluralists, and others only local loyalists) seem to believe, then closure must be permitted somewhere. At some level of political organization, something like the sovereign state must take shape and claim the authority to make its own admissions policy, to control and sometimes restrain the flow of immigrants" (ibid., 39).

There is a quick slide in this passage from "the value of the distinctiveness of cultures and groups" to the need for closure and to the justification for "something like the sovereign state" to control boundaries and set admissions policies. Walzer does not distinguish between the methodological fiction of a unitary "cultural community" and the institutional polity. A democratic polity with pluralist traditions consists of many cultural groups and subgroups, many cultural traditions and countertraditions; furthermore the "national" culture itself is formed by the contested multiplicity of many traditions, narratives and historical appropriations. All this Walzer would hardly deny (see Walzer 2001). But why exactly then is closure necessary to maintain the distinctiveness of cultures and groups?

I want to distinguish between *cultural integration* and *political integration* and to suggest that in robust liberal democracies the porousness of borders is not a threat to, but rather an enrichment of, existing democratic diversity. Cultural communities are built around their members' adherence to values, norms, and traditions that bear a *prescriptive* value for their identity, in that failure to comply with them affects their own understandings of membership and belonging. Surely, though, there is always contestation and innovation around such cultural definitions and narratives: what does it mean to be an observant but a non-orthodox Jew? What does it mean to be a modern Muslim woman? What does it mean to be a pro-choice Catholic? Cultural traditions consist of such narratives of interpretation and reinterpretation, appropriation and subversion. The more alive a cultural tradition, the more contestation there will be about its core elements (Benhabib 2002a). Walzer invokes a "we." This "we" suggests an identity without conflict, a unity without "fissure." It is a convenient methodological fiction, but its consequences for political argument can be invidious.

Political integration refers to those practices and rules, constitutional traditions and institutional habits, that bring individuals together to form a functioning political community. This functioning has a twofold dimension: not only must it be possible to run the economy, the state, and its administrative apparatus, but there must also be a dimension of belief in the *legitimacy* of the major institutions of societies in doing so. The legal-rational authority of the modern state rests not only on administrative and economic efficiency but also on a belief in its legitimacy. Precisely because modern states presuppose a plurality of competing as well as coexisting worldviews, principles of political integration are necessarily more abstract and more generalizable than principles of cultural identity. In the modern state, political life is one sphere of existence among many others with their multiple claims upon us; the disjunction between personal identities and personal allegiances, public choices and private involvements, is constitutive of the freedom of citizens in liberal democracies.

Of course, there will be some variation across existing political communities as to the constituents of such political integration: the typology of civic and ethnic nationalism indicates such a range (Cesarani and Fulbrook 1996). Nonetheless, in liberal democracies *conceptions of human and citizens' rights, constitutional traditions as well as democratic practices of election and representation,* are the *core* normative elements of political integration. It is toward them that citizens as well as foreigners, nationals as well as resident aliens, have to show respect and loyalty, and not toward any specific cultural tradition.

Precisely because Walzer conflates cultural with political integration (in the *Spheres of Justice* at least),[18] many of his wise claims about immigration and naturalization policy give the impression that they are the results of what Kant would call "contracts of beneficence." These policies remain unconstrained by a robust understanding of human rights and in the final analysis seem to rest more on the moral good will and political generosity of the democratic people alone, rather than upon principles. To be sure, such good will and political generosity are crucial to the culture of democratic legitimacy in any policy, but Walzer leaves unclear what constraints, if any, ought to be placed upon the will of democratic majorities.

Walzer does not thematize the dual, fractured identity of the members of the modern democratic sovereign

[18] In an exchange we had in *The Responsive Community*, Michael Walzer strenuously rejected that he had made this conflation and defended pluralism. But the logic of the argument in *Spheres of Justice* does not permit a robust differentiation between political integration and the cultural-ethnic identity.

Walzer, in his response to me, defends the right of democratic nations to pass anti-foreign and anti-immigration legislation on the basis that they are thereby exercising self-determination (Walzer 2001). I do not question that democratic nations may do so. My question is what do political philosophers think and do when democratic nations do so. Why are we so willing to accept that the "good Danes" (Walzer's example) may pass xenophobic and anti-immigration legislation while condemning Hitler's denaturalization of German-Jewish citizens upon coming to power? What are the criteria that we use to find the first acceptable and the second odious? See Benhabib 2001a and Walzer's response (2001). See Benhabib 2001b for further discussion.

as bearers of human rights qua moral persons on the one hand, and as bearers of citizens' rights and members of the sovereign on the other. In his view, the dualism between universal human rights principles and the exigencies of sovereign self-determination are eliminated in favor of the right to collective self-determination. Repeatedly, citizens' identity is given a thick cultural coating, while human rights are treated as being merely contextual.

In a passage remarkably reminiscent of Edmund Burke's critique of the French Revolution, Walzer writes: "Men and women do indeed have rights beyond life and liberty, but these do not follow from our common humanity; they follow from shared conceptions of social goods; they are local and particular in character" (1983, xv). We may indeed wish to ask how a shared conception of "social goods" is to provide a conception of rights, since it is rights claims which, more often than not, are invoked to arbitrate among conflicting conceptions of social goods.

The democratic people constitute themselves as sovereign because they uphold certain principles of human rights and because the terms of their association interpret as well as flesh out these rights. Of course, the precise interpretation of human rights and the content of citizens' rights must be spelled out and articulated in light of the concrete historical traditions and practices of a given society. Yet these principles are not exhausted, either in their validity or in their content, through their embodiment in specific cultural and legal traditions alone. They have a context-transcending validity claim, in the name of which the excluded and the downtrodden, the marginalized and the despised, mobilize and claim political agency and membership. The history of democratic reforms and revolutions, from the workers' movements to the suffragists, from anti-discrimination to anti-colonial struggles, widen the circle of addressees of these rights, as well as transforming their content. It is precisely because these rights have a context-transcending quality that they can be invoked by those who have been excluded "from shared conceptions of social goods" and for whom the "local and the particular" have borne stigmata of inequality, oppression, and marginalization. In the final analysis, human rights become the thinnest of moral reeds in Walzer's seemingly sturdy thicket of cultural ties and bonds.

David Jacobson is more explicit about the deleterious effects of a regime of migration, refugee, and asylum rights upon the nation-state. The growth of an international human rights regime and the spread of international norms constraining the will of sovereign states in immigration as well as refugee and asylum matters dwarf the nation-state in less than salutary ways (Jacobson 1997). Jacobson's concern is voiced in various forms: first there is the argument that too much and too quick an absorption of foreigners into a polity can change the nature of that polity by overwhelming it; under such conditions, states should have a right to protect their cultural identities. Second, to prevent one's cultural identity from being diluted, states can make *either conditions of entry or conditions of access* to citizenship quite difficult. There is no moral obligation to facilitate naturalization. A third strategy is to diminish the social and economic entitlements and benefits of foreigners – be they immigrants, refugees, or asylees – already living in the country such that the incentive to remain within a country or to seek entry into it is greatly reduced.

One or another of these arguments, and often all three in combination, are frequently heard in everyday politics. Both the United States and the member states of the European Union have restricted their entry and absorption policies in recent years by adopting many such measures. For example, while the 1996 Immigration Reform Act in the USA speeded up the process of granting citizenship to illegal immigrants, that same year the US Congress also enacted a bill that denied certain welfare benefits, including food stamps and financial support for the aged and the disabled, to all immigrants, whether legal or illegal. This law, passed on August 22, 1996, was unusual in its severity in that it applied even to those who were admitted into the USA before that date; a year later it was rescinded, and in June 1998 food stamps were restored to children, the elderly, and the disabled who had entered the USA prior to August 1996.

One of the most compelling arguments against such draconian measures of sovereign self-expression has been put forward by Owen Fiss. Fiss suggests that, evaluated within the context of American constitutional traditions, these policies "raise with special urgency and clarity the question whether enactments imposing social disabilities on immigrants can be squared with the Constitution, particularly the provision that guarantees to all persons – not all citizens, but all persons – equal protection of the laws" (1998, 4). Building upon trans-formations of US immigration law from a model of sovereign privilege to one that accepts international human rights norms as binding upon the will of legislatures and the judgments of the courts, legal scholars Peter Schuck (1998) and Gerald Neuman (1996) have demonstrated why contemporary debates around these issues can no longer be framed primarily in terms of the cultural identities of receiving countries; they center on the rights claims of migrants as well.[19] The status of alienage is no longer denuded of rights. Aliens enjoy not only human rights but also considerable civil and political rights in the countries of which they are residents. They can challenge decisions of immigration authorities to deport them and to hold them without counsel. Alienage is increasingly a status protected by the courts, a status which is coming under "strict scrutiny" in cases of discrimination even against illegal aliens.

The decline-of-citizenship school proceeds from an impoverished model of democratic identity as ethnocultural commonality as well as minimizing the divisiveness of the debate within liberal democracies concerning migration. Focusing on one aspect of an idealized model of citizenship alone, that of shared language and cultural heritage, they neglect the institutional spaces within which *the dialectic of political rights and cultural identities* unfolds. Precisely because migrations, whatever their causes, pose such fundamental challenges to the self-understanding of liberal-democratic peoples, it is simply empirically false to assume, as the decline-of-citizenship theorists do, that shared cultural commonalities will always trump human rights claims. Rather, what we see

---

[19] The immigration debate in the USA has been radically changed by the events of September 11, 2001, and by the wars in Afghanistan and Iraq. In the aftermath of these events, immigration has become increasingly criminalized. As Ronald Dworkin has written with respect to the USA Patriot Act, which was passed by Congress on October 25, 2001, it proceeds from a "breathtakingly vague and broad definition of terrorism and of aiding terrorism"(Dworkin 2002). It also relaxes rules that protect people suspected of crime from unfair investigation and prosecution.

are internally fractured political communities which continue to negotiate the terms of their own collective identities at the site of migration debates.

The following chapter begins with a discourse-theoretic analysis of rights claims and proceeds to a sociological case study of the transformations of citizenship practices in contemporary Europe. As opposed to globalists, I want to show that redistributive questions affect membership in subtle and interesting ways: for example, although guest workers entered European countries throughout the 1950s and 1960s in search of economic arrangements which were mutually beneficial to both the receiving countries and the migrants themselves, these arrangements alone did not lead to the emergence of liberalized citizenship politics until much later in the evolution of the European rights regime. Practices and institutions of just membership cannot be reduced to matters of redistributive justice, although the two are interrelated.

Communitarians are right to argue against globalists that local democratic conditions are crucial to any membership debate. What they neglect, in turn, and which my case study of European transformations of citizenship is intended to show, is the crucial interdependence of rights and identities, of political institutions and cultural communities. The expansion of the European rights regime integrated guest workers into the legal, political, and cultural systems of their host countries, giving rise in turn to a dynamic toward political integration – that is, formal citizenship acquisition.

The phenomenon of migration, along with the predicament of asylum seekers and refugees in the contemporary world, thus touches upon some of the deepest interests and passions in liberal-democratic societies. While universalists and cosmopolitans judge the closed-door policies of the wealthy nations of Europe and North America to be forms of organized hypocrisy that will not bear closer philosophical scrutiny, decline-of-citizenship theorists point to values such as the rule of law, a vibrant civic culture, and active citizenship, which are equally important to such societies and which they consider to be threatened by worldwide migrations.

In this chapter I have argued that migration and crossborder justice cannot be addressed through distributive measures alone. Concurring with decline-of-citizenship theorists that democratic self-governance is a fundamental political good, I have nevertheless questioned their visions of ethical and political integration. I have argued that their perspective on the dialectic of rights and identities, within the framework of which migratory movements and crossborder justice must be treated, is inadequate. To develop this framework will be the task of the next two chapters.

4

Transformations of citizenship: the European Union

A non-foundationalist human rights discourse

So far I have used the concept of human rights without much elucidation. I have relied on Kantian moral premises to explicate the philosophical strategy behind the right of hospitality. In my discussion of the ambivalences of Arendt's concept of rights, I have also distinguished between the *moral* and the *juridico-civil* sense of the term. I have followed this strategy in part because I have sought to clarify the internal contradictions of the normative commitments of liberal democracies. What is the status of rights within a discourse theory of ethics? Can a discourse-ethical justification of rights claims lead us beyond the impasses that usually afflict "rights talk"?

Since Jeremy Bentham's quip that belief in natural rights is "nonsense on stilts" (1843, II, 501), rights claims have been mistaken to refer to certain moral properties or attributes of human beings. The language of "natural rights" perpetrated the naturalistic fallacy in that it conflated a claim about moral grounds – the reasons why we ought to recognize each others' claims to action or forbearance, resources or services of certain sorts – with a seeming description of the physical and psychological attributes of existing moral entities – that individuals could not but act in pursuit of self-preservation (Hobbes) or

I wish to thank Willem Maas for his extremely helpful comments on an earlier draft of this chapter.

for the protection of their life, liberty, and property (Locke). Natural rights talk, as found in the writings of Hobbes, Locke, and Rousseau, vacillated between psychological truisms such as "each living being tends to its self-preservation" and moral injunctions of the kind, "seek Peace, and follow it" (Hobbes [1651] 1966, 92). Historically the widespread use of the terms *property* and *propriety* to designate rights claims in general served to demarcate a sphere of individual claims and entitlements and gave them an aspect of inviolability (see Tuck 1979).

Being deeply shaped by an emergent capitalist commodity economy which was fast transforming all human goods and resources into saleable property, the political imaginary of natural rights theories readily reduced rights-talk to property-talk. Property rights themselves came to be viewed as paradigmatic, although, as G. W. F. Hegel noted sarcastically with respect to Locke and Hobbes, the irony in this conflation was that, unlike property rights, the natural rights to life and liberty were not alienable and could not be commodified (Hegel [1821] 1973; Benhabib 1984). Far from being reducible to property rights, the individual could be recognized as a rights-bearing person only insofar as his rights to life and liberty were not saleable property.

We need repeat neither the naturalistic fallacy nor the paradigmatic uses of property to illustrate rights claims. I will assume that rights claims are in general of the following sort: "I can justify to you with good grounds that you and I should respect each others' reciprocal claims to act in certain ways and not to act in others, and to enjoy certain resources and services."

130

In his *Metaphysics of Morals*, Kant proposes that there is one basic right – "Every action which by itself or by its maxim enables the freedom of each individual's will to coexist with the freedom of everyone else in accordance with a universal law is *right* [*gerecht*]" (Kant [1797] 1996, 133). Note that this formulation is not about a list of basic rights which is said to precede the will of the republican sovereign. Rather, this principle establishes how a juridico-civil order can come into existence which would be in compliance with the moral law. The "principle of right," like the traditional discourse of natural rights, basically states that only that political order is legitimate which is based upon a system of general laws that binds the will of each equally. *Generality* and *formal reciprocity* are features of the rule of law, of a political order based upon the idea of the *Rechtstaat*.

Does this Kantian clarification, and I would say improvement, of rights discourse rest upon metaphysical premises? Is the Kantian principle of *right* – the idea of political power as based upon moral respect for persons under the rule of law – marred by metaphysical commitments? Do the metaphysical dualisms of his moral philosophy also affect Kant's doctrine of right and justice? A concern of this kind was also behind Hannah Arendt's skepticism that one could successfully justify "the right to have rights" ([1951] 1968, 298–299).

A postmetaphysical justification of the principle of right would differ from Kant's in the following way: instead of asking what each could will without self-contradiction to be a universal law for all, in discourse ethics we ask which norms and normative institutional arrangements would be considered valid by all those who would be affected if they were participants in special moral argumentations called discourses. The emphasis now shifts from what each can will via a thought-experiment to be valid for all, to those justificatory processes through which you and I in dialogue, and with good reasons, can convince each other of the validity of certain norms – by which I mean simply "general rules of action." The link between the Kantian legacy of treating human beings as ends and never merely as means and this discursive principle of justification has been succintly stated by Thomas Nagel: "If you force someone to serve an end that he cannot be given adequate reason to share, you are treating him as a mere means – even if the end is his own good, as you see it but he doesn't" (1991, 159).

Whether or not such a postmetaphysical reformulation of the Kantian principle of right via discourse ethics succeeds may be claimed to depend on what one means by "good reasons," by "rational discourse," and the like. The objection to discourse ethics is that it begs the question, i.e., that engages in *petitio principii*. This is an important objection and I have dealt with it a decade ago in *Situating the Self* (1992). I cannot say that my efforts have put this objection to rest, but let me reiterate here why restating the principle of right in terms of a discourse theory of moral justification does not beg all the relevant questions.

Recall that we are not concerned with the domain of the moral at large in this discussion. My question is whether a postmetaphysical justification of rights discourse is possible. The brief answer is that: "If I am able to justify to you why it is right that you and I should act in certain ways, then I must respect your capacity to agree or disagree with me on the basis of reasons which equally apply to us both. But to respect your capacity for communicative freedom – to accept or reject on the basis of reasons – means to respect your capacity for personal autonomy. Human rights, or basic rights, then, are the norms that would undergird and enable the exercise of your personal autonomy." Note that in this formulation I am avoiding giving any substantive content to "good reasons," or even specifying what cognitive, psychological, or other attributes we must attribute to persons in order to consider them capable of discursive justification. Nor am I claiming that discursive justification exhausts the moral domain – for obviously we have moral obligations to those who cannot enter into discourses with us (see pp. 13–14 above). I am claiming that even those norms whose origins may lie outside discursive processes ought to be discursively justifiable, when and if called into question.

Basic rights or human rights are conditions that enable the exercise of personal autonomy; first and foremost as a moral being you have a fundamental *right to justification* (Forst 1999). Your freedom can be restricted only through reciprocally and generally justifiable norms which equally apply to all. In the sphere of morality, generality means *universality*; universality refers to what would be valid for all human beings considered as beings equally entitled to respect and concern – what I have named in *Situating the Self* (1992) *egalitarian reciprocity*.

How, if at all, can one make the transition from these highly abstract and formal considerations of the basic right to communicative freedom to the specific rights regimes, legal systems, charters, and conventions of existing polities? The discourse of liberal democracies is necessarily caught in this tension created by the context- and community-transcending

133

validity dimension of human rights on the one hand, and the historically formed, culturally generated, and socially shaped specificities of existing juridico-civil communities on the other. The point is not to deny this tension by embracing only one or another of these moral alternatives but to negotiate their interdependence, by resituating or reiterating the universal in concrete contexts. If we identify the moral universal with the juridico-civil, we end up with more or less benign forms of communitarianism or ethical relativism; if we ignore the juridico-political and the permissible range of variations in different systems and traditions (what I referred to above as the *schedule of rights*), we dismiss the political in the name of the moral.

The human right to membership

Does the communicative reformulation of basic or human rights help us resolve the puzzles which Kant and Arendt were struggling with? Kant could not bridge the gap between the right of temporary visitation and the right of permanent residency; Arendt saw the practice of denaturalization and the condition of statelessness as being almost equivalent to the loss of rights altogether. She could offer no solution to this predicament other than the founding of new human communities which would guarantee membership to the stateless and the dispossessed. Since every new polity only reproduced the dilemma between insiders and outsiders, those who were full citizens and those who were not, it is hard to see why this practice alone would solve the problems she was posing.

Since the end of World War II some of Arendt's concerns, who was herself a stateless person between 1935 and 1941, have been addressed institutionally. The 1948 Universal Declaration of Human Rights forbids *arbitrary denaturalization*,[1] i.e., the loss of one's citizenship status, and considers the loss of nationality to be a violation of basic human rights. Regrettably, newly forming nation-states in processes of decolonization have copiously engaged in this practice since the mid-1960s. They need to be told loudly and clearly by the world community that, no matter what the wounds of colonization may have been, there are ways to redress economic, social, and cultural inequities other than by rendering people stateless. Liberal democracies that would condemn decolonizing nations for these practices must themselves accept naturalization, i.e., admittance to citizenship, as the obverse side of the injunction against denaturalization. Just as you cannot render individuals stateless at will, nor can you, as a sovereign state, deny them membership in perpetuity. You may stipulate certain criteria of membership, but they can never be of such a kind that others would be permanently barred from becoming a member of your polity. Theocratic, authoritarian, fascist, and nationalist regimes do this, but liberal democracies ought not to.

[1] The language of Article 15 of the Universal Declaration of Human Rights (United Nations 1948) reads: "No one shall be arbitrarily deprived of his nationality nor denied the right to change his nationality." This permits sovereign states some latitude in determining what would be "non-arbitrary" denaturalization. In this book, I am questioning some of the standard practices which states, wishing to promote nationalist and ethnocentric majorities, may themselves deem non-arbitrary.

I want to argue that the basic human right to communicative freedom enables us both to justify the *human right to membership* and to interdict *loss of membership* or denaturalization.

Let me distinguish first the various phases of migration, of the geographical movement of peoples across state boundaries to settle in countries other than those of their birth. Migration involves *emigration* (the first causes and conditions of departure); actual *first entry* into a foreign country; civil, economic, and cultural *absorption* of a shorter or longer duration (visitation, business, study); *incorporation*, that is, residency of a significant duration; and finally *naturalization*, i.e., access to political citizenship. The liberal tradition has long assumed that the right to leave one's country of origin is a fundamental, even if an imperfect natural right. Thus Locke writes that "The only way whereby any one divests himself of his natural liberty, and puts on the *bonds of civil society*, is by agreeing with other men to join and unite into a community" (Locke [1690] 1980, 52). Thomas Jefferson gives this a more striking formulation when he refers to it as the "right which nature has given to all men of departing from the country in which chance, not choice has placed them" (Jefferson [1774] 1984, 4). For the liberal tradition, this right to depart or to emigrate is a basic right, itself grounded upon the view of the human person as an autonomous being entitled to accept or reject with reasons those basic preconditions of the exercise of his or her communicative freedom. Certainly, the choice of one's country of residence is one of those fundamental preconditions. Citizens are not prisoners of their respective states. Not only must they be free to leave at will, but also no liberal state should make conditions of exit impossible by denying passports and exit visas or by imposing exorbitant exit fees. Furthermore, no state has the right to interdict reentry to an expatriate to the territory upon which he or she was born. If the individual in question has not voluntarily abdicated his/her citizenship, there must be procedures for regaining one's previous citizenship. These obligations of the liberal-democratic state toward its citizens derive from the principle that the citizens of such a union are to be viewed as legal consociates entitled to the basic exercise of their communicative freedom, and fundamental to this communicative freedom is the right to withdraw consent to exist within certain state boundaries.

Of course this manner of presenting the problem is refracted through the highly individualistic premises of social-contract theory: the reasons for migration are rarely simply personal or idiosyncratic. In the majority of cases, the root causes of migration are poverty, famine, and persecution on the basis of race, religion, ethnicity, language, gender, and sexual preference, as well as ethnocide, genocide, civil wars, earth-quakes, pestilence, and the like. These events create refugees and asylees as well as migrants. Clearly, first-admission conditions for immigrants are of a different sort from those for refugees and asylum seekers. States have more discretion to stipulate conditions of entry in the case of immigration than they do when facing refugees and asylees. Their obligations to the latter groups are moral and, for those states who are signatories to the Geneva Convention on the Status of Refugees (United Nations 1951) and its 1967 Protocol they are legal.

Once first admission occurs, what is the obligation of a liberal state to those it has admitted? Is there a human right to membership? I want to argue that there is and that this right is the obverse of the interdiction against denaturalization. From the standpoint of discourse theory, the moral argument would have to proceed as follows: "If you and I enter into a moral dialogue with one another, and I am a member of a state of which you are seeking membership and you are not, then I must be able to show you with good grounds, with grounds that would be acceptable to each of us equally, why you can never join our association and become one of us. These must be grounds that you would accept if you were in my situation and I were in yours. Our reasons must be reciprocally acceptable; they must apply to each of us equally." Are there such grounds that would be reciprocally acceptable? Clearly, reasons that barred you from membership because of the *kind* of being you were, your ascriptive and non-elective attributes such as your race, gender, religion, ethnicity,[2] language community,

---

[2] Ethnicity has always been considered a significant factor in denying or enabling admission to citizenship. States in which certain ethnic groups reside are likely to plead for special treatment of their ethnic kin; in fact, there are states, such as Israel, which make the right of return a legal privilege for those who can claim Jewish descent. Similarly, Germany has policies which grant special privileges of return to ethnic Germans from the Baltic states, Russia, and other countries of eastern and central Europe (the so-called *Aussiedler* and *Vertriebene*). As long as a state does not deny those of different ethnicity and religion equivalent rights to seek entry and admission into a country, I think that these practices need not be discriminatory. It is only because such practices are combined with the goals of preserving ethnic majorities and ethnic purity that they run afoul of and are discriminatory from a human rights perspective. Israel's "law of return," for example, violates the human rights of Palestinian refugees, many of whom by now may not even be interested in returning to Israel and who may be willing to agree to various other forms of compensation.

or sexuality, would not be permissible, because I would then be reducing your capacity to exercise communicative freedom to those characteristics which were given to you by chance or accident and which you did not choose. (Historically, religious conversion was always considered a venue for accepting outsiders into the commonwealth, and was thus not viewed as an ascriptive but as an elective attribute.) No reasons that would bar certain groups of individuals from membership permanently because of the kinds of human beings they were could be reciprocally acceptable. However, criteria that stipulate that you must show certain qualifications, skills, and resources to become a member are permissible because they do not deny your communicative freedom. Length of stay, language competence, a certain proof of civic literacy, demonstration of material resources, or marketable skills are all conditions which certainly can be abused in practice, but which, from the standpoint of normative theory, do not violate the self-understanding of liberal democracies as associations which respect the communicative freedom of human beings qua human beings.

This right to membership entails *a right to know* on the part of the foreigner who is seeking membership: how can

Still others may be able to prove with good grounds that they fall under the family-unification clause of various refugee conventions, and therefore must be admitted into Israel. Alas, a recent decision of the Israeli Cabinet rescinded even the right of Palestinians who had married Israeli citizens to attain Israeli citizenship, thereby violating one of the fundamental clauses of international law – namely the unification of families caught on different sides of borders. Germany, by contrast, avoided the ethnocentric nationalism of its policies vis-à-vis the "expellees," by liberalizing its citizenship laws and permitting immigration to all who met certain qualifications.

139

conditions of naturalization be fulfilled? The answer to this question must be made publicly available to all, transparent in its formulations, and not be subject to bureaucratic capriciousness. There must be a clear procedure, administered in lawful fashion, through which naturalization can occur and there must be a right of appeal in the event of a negative outcome, as there would be in most civil cases. One must not criminalize the immigrant and the foreigner; one must safeguard their right to due process, to representation in one's language, and the right to independent counsel.

The human right to membership straddles two broad categories: human rights and civil and political rights. I am arguing that the *entitlement* to all civil rights – including rights to association, property, and contract – and eventually to political rights, must itself be considered a human right. This suggests that the sovereign discretion of the democratic community is circumscribed: once admission occurs, the path to membership ought not to be blocked. Kant's distinction between the temporary right of sojourn and the longer-term right of visitation can no longer be sustained (see ch. 1 above), since from a discourse-theoretic point of view I cannot justify to you with good grounds why you should remain a permanent stranger upon the land. This would amount to a denial of your communicative freedom and moral personality.

A serious objection can be raised against this line of argument: to insist that the right to membership – that is, to naturalization – follows from a discourse-ethical standpoint seems to bind the will of the democratic sovereign in accordance with a specific concretization of rights. But would you not thereby be imposing a *specific schedule of rights* upon democratic will-formation processes? What amount of democratic variation in rights schedules is compatible with discourse-theoretical premises? I had introduced above a distinction between the *principle of rights* and a *schedule of rights* which would be determined by each democratic sovereign. Can the human right to membership be considered a violation of this distinction?

If one understood by the human right to membership the specific content of the right to citizenship in a specific polity, then one could plausibly argue that such a right ought not to be considered a moral or basic human right but a political or citizen's right. Instead I am suggesting that the human right to membership is more general than the specific citizenship legislation of this or that country. Some polities may require a written language exam to prove competence, others may be satisfied with an oral demonstration alone; some countries may require a residency of seven years, others may be satisfied with three. Some may grant permanent residents the right to vote in municipal elections, as is the case with the Netherlands, the United Kingdom, and Ireland; others, such as Germany, may permit the vote only after naturalization. These are variations within the power and prerogative of the democratic people. What would be objectionable from a moral point of view is the absence of *any* procedure or possibility for foreigners and resident aliens to become citizens at all; that is, if naturalization were not permitted at all, or if it were restricted on the basis of religious, ethnic, racial, and sexual preference grounds, this would violate the human right to membership. In this sense, the human right to membership is an aspect of the *principle of right, i.e., of the recognition of the individual as a being who is entitled to moral respect, a being whose communicative freedom we must recognize.*[3]

The human right to membership is not merely an abstract moral "ought" but is increasingly incorporated into existing rights regimes through various practices and institutions. The margin of divergence with respect not only to human rights but also to civil and political rights is diminishing in many liberal democracies. The sovereign privilege of naturalization appears increasingly as a relic from a bygone era of statist supremacy. Given the level of integration of non-nationals

---

[3] Does the human right to membership rest on a problematic distinction between "voluntarily chosen" identity attributes such as one's profession, and "ascribed" or "non-voluntary" characteristics such as one's language group, ethnicity, religion, etc.? And, if so, wouldn't one be taking a rather essentialist view of these latter identity features? I have argued against such cultural essentialism at length in Benhabib 2002a, 1–23, and do not consider such essentialism central to my claim about the human right to membership at all. Rather, I am maintaining that citizens in liberal democracies view themselves as possessing concrete identities as well as being the bearers of universal moral and political rights. Denying foreigners and residents the right to become citizens of liberal democracies on a permanent basis violates the communicative freedom of all persons inherent in the understanding of these rights, and is hypocritical as well as self-contradictory. So the question bears on the balance between the shared, public culture of liberal democracies and the specific cultural, linguistic, and religious legacies of peoples. What is the relationship between the *demos* and the *ethnos*? I suggest that a permanent ban on the naturalization of others is incompatible with a liberal democracy. Such regimes would become authoritarian and eventually oppressive "ethnocracies." I do not believe in the concept of an "ethnic democracy," which is current in some contemporary discussions in Israel in particular. I return to this in chapter 5 below. Many thanks to Patchen Markell for bringing this objection to my attention.

and non-citizens into rights regimes, national citizenship has ceased to be the sole basis for the ascription of rights.

In what follows, I will consider the transformation of the institutions of citizenship in contemporary Europe. Contemporary institutional developments point in contradictory directions. On the one hand they affirm the significance of national citizenship; at the same time they minimize the distinction between the legal status of citizens and aliens. These developments have led to the disaggregation of the unitary model of citizenship into its component elements.

The inclusion of this case study shifts the terrain of the argument from a normative-analytical to an institutional-sociological perspective. I do not mean to suggest thereby that empirical developments alone can resolve the normative dilemmas of membership rights; however, it is important for political philosophy to take stock of concrete trends and transformations. In doing so, I am following the example of Hegel's *Philosophy of Right*, which tried to situate freedom in the world of "objective Spirit" ([1821] 1973). Through an internal critique of the contradictory potentials of institutions which frame our lives, we gain a clearer understanding of our rights and freedoms. There is no teleology of reconciliation promised by my considerations, as there was in Hegelian philosophy; nor can the moral "ought" be reduced to the institutional "is." Yet it is my belief that we will better appreciate the contradictory nature of the present if we have a clearer sense of actual institutional transformations in the domain of membership rights. For too long normative political theory and the political sociology of the modern state have gone their separate ways. This book is a plea for their fruitful collaboration.

A sociological mode of citizenship rights

Citizenship in the modern world has meant membership in a bounded political community which was either a nation-state, a multinational state, or a commonwealth structure. The political regime of territorially bounded sovereignty, exercised through formal-rational administrative procedures and dependent upon the democratic will-formation of a more or less culturally homogeneous group of people, could only function by defining, circumscribing, and controlling citizenship. The citizen is the individual who has membership rights to reside within a territory, who is subject to the state's administrative jurisdiction, and who is also, ideally, a member of the democratic sovereign in the name of whom laws are issued and administration is exercised. Following Max Weber, we may say that this *unity of residency, administrative subjection, democratic participation, and cultural membership* constitutes the "ideal typical" model of citizenship in the modern nation-state of the West (see Weber [1956] 1978, 901–926). The influence of this model, whether or not it adequately corresponds to local conditions, extends far beyond the West: modernizing nations in Africa, the Middle East, and Asia, which entered the process of state-formation at later points than their west European counterparts, copied this model wherever they came into existence as well.

What is the status of citizenship today, in a world of increasingly deterritorialized politics? How is citizenship being reconfigured under contemporary conditions? How has the fraying of the four functions of the state – territoriality, administrative control, democratic legitimacy, and cultural identity – affected the theory and practice of citizenship?

The practice and institution of citizenship can be disaggregated into three components: collective identity, privileges of political membership, and social rights and claims. While political theorists tend to focus primarily on the privileges of political membership, social scientists and social historians have been more interested in the formation of collective identities and the evolution of rights claims associated with the status of citizenship (Benhabib 2002a, 162–171).

The view that citizenship is a status that confers upon one entitlements and benefits as well as obligations derives from T. H. Marshall (1950). Marshall's catalogue of civil, political, and social rights is modeled upon the cumulative logic of struggles for expanding democracy in the nineteenth and early part of the twentieth century. "Civil rights" arise with the birth of the absolutist state, and in their earliest and most basic form they entail the rights to the protection of life, liberty, and property, the right to freedom of conscience, and certain associational rights, such as those of commerce and marriage.

"Political rights" in the narrow sense refer to the rights of self-determination, to hold and run for office, to establish political and non-political associations, including a free press and free institutions of science and culture. "Social rights" are last in Marshall's catalogue; they were achieved historically through the struggles of the workers', women's, and other social movements of the past two centuries. Social rights entail the right to form trade unions as well as other professional and trade associations, health care rights, unemployment compensation, old age pensions, child care, housing, and educational subsidies. These social rights vary widely across countries and depend on the social class compromises prevalent in any given welfare-state democracy (Soysal 1994). Their inclusion in any internationally agreed-upon catalogue of universal human rights – beyond the mere right to employment and a decent standard of living – is a bone of contention among different countries with different economic outlooks.

I want to illustrate this disaggregation effect with reference to the rights regimes of the contemporary European Union, in which the rights of citizens of member countries of the EU are sharply delineated from those of third-country nationals, within a patchwork of local, national, and supranational rights regimes. The unitary model, which combined continuous residency upon a given territory with a shared national identity, the enjoyment of political rights, and subjection to a common administrative jurisdiction, is coming apart. One can have one set of rights but not another: one can have political rights without being a national, as is the case for EU nationals; more commonly, though, one has social rights and benefits, by virtue of being a foreign worker, without either sharing in the same collective identity or having the privileges of political membership. The danger in this situation is that of "permanent alienage," namely the creation of a group in society that partakes of property rights and civil society without having access to political rights.[4]

---

[4] Parts of this discussion have previously appeared in Benhabib 2002b.

Citizenship in contemporary Europe

According to the "Treaty Establishing a Constitution for Europe" (2003, which still needs to be ratified by member states) and following upon the Treaty of Maastricht (1992), "Every national of a Member State shall be a citizen of the Union. Citizenship of the Union shall be additional to national citizenship; it shall not replace it."[5] Nationals of all countries who are members of the European Union – Austria, Belgium, Cyprus, the Czech Republic, Denmark, Estonia, Finland, France, Germany, Greece, Hungary, Ireland, Italy, Latvia, Lithuania, Luxembourg, Malta, the Netherlands, Poland, Portugal, Slovakia, Slovenia, Spain, Sweden, and the UK – are also citizens of the European Union. What does being a citizen of the EU mean? What privileges and responsibilities, what rights and duties, does this entitle one to? Is citizenship of the union merely a status category, just as membership of the Roman Empire[6] was? Does membership in the union amount

---

[5] See Article I-8 of "Treaty Establishing a Constitution for Europe," (european-convention.eu.int/docs/Treaty/cv00820.en03.pdf); the original formulation from the Treaty of Maastricht, Article 8 of C. Part Two, reads: "1. Citizenship of the Union is hereby established. Every Person holding the Nationality of a Member State shall be a citizen of the Union" (facsimile reproduction on file with the author). A more extensive discussion of these issues appears in Benhabib, 2002a, ch. 6.

[6] By referring to Roman citizenship in this context, I am recalling some of the civic republican criticisms of the extension of Roman *civitas* to provincial elites and those who served in the military. As Rome conquered more peoples and territories, Roman citizenship lost its hereditary character and became more territorial. With the rise of the empire, the franchise lost its significance. From Machiavelli to the young Hegel, to Edward Gibbon, the extension of Roman *civitas* and the decline

to more than possessing a passport that allows one to pass through the correct doors at border crossings?[7]

Clearly, union membership is intended to be more than that. Not just a passive status, it is also intended to designate an active civic identity. Citizens of EU states can settle anywhere in the union, take up jobs in their chosen countries, and vote as well as stand for office in local elections and in elections for the Parliament of Europe.[8] They have the right to enjoy consular and diplomatic representation in the

of the republic have been seen to go hand in hand. Contemporary historian Michael Mann argues that the invention of extensive territorial citizenship also gave Rome an edge over other entities such as Carthage. See Mann 1986, 254.

In this context, I only mean to signal that the *topos* of the transition from republic to empire and the decline of active citizenship is present in the memory of many contemporary European observers as they reflect on the transformations brought about by the European Union. I wish to thank Willem Maas for his extremely helpful observations and suggestions on this matter.

7   The institution of citizenship among individuals who do not share a common language, a common public sphere, and effective channels of participation has given rise to a number of debates in political theory and jurisprudence. Some see European citizenship as a fig leaf intended to cover the considerable divestment of the democratic powers of sovereign peoples to an anonymous "Eurocracy" sitting in Brussels, and still more others warn of the growing "democracy deficit" in the union. Citizenship without participation looms on the horizon, they argue. See Preuss 1995; Balibar 1996; Lehning and Weale 1997. This case has been made most recently and forcefully by Weiler 1999.

8   This chapter was concluded during the accession of the EU of ten new member states in the spring of 2004. The mobility rights of citizens of these new members to assume residency and jobs in the territory of the former fifteen EU member states have been restricted for a period up to seven years. At the present time, it is also unclear what the final regulation

territory of a third country in which the member state whose nationals they are may not be represented. They have the right to petition the European Parliament and to apply to the European Ombudsman (Treaty of the Constitution, Article I-8-2, european-convention.eu.int/docs/Treaty/cv00820.en03.pdf). As European monetary and economic integration progresses, EU members are debating whether union citizenship should be extended to an equivalent package of social rights and benefits, such as unemployment compensation, health care, and old age pensions, which members of EU states would be able to enjoy whichever EU country they take up residency in.

The obverse side of membership in the EU is a sharper delineation of the conditions of those who are non-members. The agreements of Schengen and Dublin intended to make practices of granting asylum and refugee status throughout member states uniform.[9] Referred to as "legal harmonization," in the early 1990s, these agreements made the acquisition of refugee and asylum status in the union increasingly difficult.[10] The Treaty of Amsterdam, agreed on June 17, 1997, placed naturalization, immigration, refugee, and asylum policies within the EU in the Third Pillar of European Law and initiated the "open method of coordination." The First Pillar refers to

of interstate mobility rights, in accordance with criteria of economic self-sufficiency, health insurance, and welfare policy, will be.

[9] See Neuman 1993. The Dublin Convention and the second Schengen agreement were signed in June 1990. Both agreements contain rules for determining a "responsible state" which agrees to process an applicant for asylum from a non-EU country.

[10] Hania Zlotnik observes that "the total number of applications lodged in European countries fell by 37 per cent between 1989–93 and 1994–98" (2001, 236).

EU-wide laws and regulations; the Second Pillar concerns common security and cooperation measures, particularly those pertaining to criminality and fighting drug-trafficking; the Third Pillar is defined as "intergovernmental law" and is subject to discretionary agreement and cooperation as well as the conventions of international public law. In these areas, a unanimous decision procedure and the open method of coordination will hold until 2004 (see de Jong 2000, 21–25). Although EU member countries retain sovereign discretion over their immigration and asylum policies, the Treaty of Amsterdam embedded immigration and asylum policies within an EU framework (van Krieken 2000, 25).

The resolutions of the European Council, reached in Tampere, Finland, on October 15–16, 1999, reiterated this commitment to European integration on the basis of respect for human rights, democratic institutions, and the rule of law. The Council emphasized that these principles ought not to be seen as the exclusive preserve of the union's own citizens. "It would be in contradiction with Europe's traditions to deny such freedoms to those whose circumstances led them justifiably to seek access to our territory. This in turn requires the union to develop common policies on asylum and immigration, while taking into account the need for a consistent control of external borders to stop illegal immigration and to combat those who organize it and commit related international crimes" (ibid., 305).

Despite these wishes for a coherent immigration and asylum policy at the intergovernmental level of EU institutions, legal and institutional conditions for immigrants and asylees vary widely among member countries. As political changes in Austria, Italy, Denmark, Portugal, Spain, and the Netherlands, which brought anti-immigration, right-wing parties to power, made amply clear throughout the late 1990s and early 2000, immigration and asylum issues remain time bombs in the hands of demagogues and right-wing politicians, ready to explode at very short notice.

The summit of the European Council ministers in Seville in June 2002 and in the aftermath of the events of September 11, 2001, gave clear indications that the declarations of Amsterdam and Tampere were at risk, and that the open method of coordination hitherto practiced in immigration, refugee, and asylum matters would be replaced by more restrictive and intolerant policies on the part of member countries.

The Presidency Conclusions of the meeting of the European Council in Thessaloniki on June 19–20, 2003, give a prominent place to "the development of a common policy on illegal migration, external borders, the return of illegal migrants and cooperation with third countries" (www.eu2003. gr/en/articles/2003/6/20/3121/). Urging the development of the Visa Information System which would coordinate the relevant information gathered from the national governments, the Council encourages the use of "biometric identifiers or biometric data, which would result in harmonised solutions for documents for third country nationals, EU citizens' passports and information systems" (ibid.). While the decision to grant or deny entry still remains with national governments, increasingly information is shared at the EU level, and procedures for granting visas are streamlined.

In an extremely important step toward creating a common European asylum system, the European Council advocates adopting "minimum standards for the qualification and status of third country nationals and stateless persons as refugees or as persons who otherwise need international protection" and the development of "minimum standards on procedures for . . . granting and withdrawing refugee status" (ibid.).

Although the Council reiterates its adherence to the 1951 Geneva Convention on Refugees and Asylum Seekers and its Protocol of 1967, the EU seeks enhanced cooperation with third countries who are sender lands in the readmission and return of their nationals who reach EU territory illegally. Cooperative efforts with sender countries to enhance border controls, to intercept illegal immigrants, and to create asylum systems have been increased. Since, in many cases, individuals seeking asylum and refuge are escaping the oppressive, illegal, and even murderous regimes of their own countries, enhanced cooperation with these governments can have disastrous effects upon their lives. A very serious danger posed by these developments is the undermining of the individual-rights-based system of the Geneva Convention and of the moral as well as constitutional obligations of individual states toward refugees and asylum seekers, in view of their own past histories of collaboration or resistance to fascism and totalitarianism, as the case may be.[11]

---

[11] In 1999–2000, the ruling Social Democratic Party–Green Coalition in Germany compromised the rather generous and liberal Law of Asylum of the German Constitution for the sake of assuring the cooperation of the conservative Christian Democratic Union and Christian Social Union in passing an immigration bill through parliament. Similar compromises were being urged in early 2004, by the Blair government in Britain. The

While admittance policies into EU member countries get stricter, for those foreigners who are already in the EU, the progress of union citizenship has given rise to discrepancies between those who are foreigners and third-country nationals, and those who are foreign nationals but EU members. A two-tiered status of foreignness has evolved: on the one hand there are third-country national foreign residents of European countries, some of whom have been born and raised in these countries and who know of no other homeland; on the other hand are those who may be near-total strangers to the language, customs, and history of their host country but who enjoy special status and privilege by virtue of being a national of an EU member state (europa.eu.int/scadplus/citizens/fr/d7.htm).

The consequence of these developments is a checkered landscape, in which not only do different practices hold in different countries, but divergent normative principles are at

British government has been planning to deport asylum seekers to new "regional processing areas" (RPAs) and "transit processing centres" (TPCs). While the former are to be located in the region of the refugee crisis, the latter are supposed to be close to the external borders of the EU. The Presidency Conclusions of the Thessaloniki EU Summit decided *not* to place proposals for transit processing centers on its agenda, but the merits of regional processing areas or protection zones, which are supported by the British and Danish governments in particular, are to be explored further. As Gregor Noll observes: "It is no exaggeration to state that it could very well mean the end of the 1951 Refugee Convention. Essentially, the British, Danish, and other supportive governments are intentionally and proactively seeking to create a permanent state of exception in the international refugee regime" ("Visions of the Exceptional," June 27, 2003, www.openDemocracynet).

work in different contexts. The disaggregation of citizenship within the EU proceeds along several axes:

(1) The entitlement to rights is no longer dependent upon the status of citizenship. Legal resident aliens have been incorporated into human rights regimes, as well as being protected by supra- and subnational legislations.

(2) The condition of undocumented resident aliens, as well as of refugees and asylum seekers, however, remains in that murky domain between legality and illegality. Until their applications have been approved, refugees and asylum seekers are not entitled freely to choose their domicile or to accept employment. A resolution to permit those whose application is still in process the right to work after three months of residency has recently been approved by the EU Council of Ministers. In some cases, children of refugees and asylees can attend school; on the whole, asylees and refugees are entitled to certain forms of medical care. Undocumented migrants, by contrast, are cut off from rights and benefits and mostly live and work clandestinely.

(3) The determination of entry conditions into member countries of the European Union, despite the declarations of the Treaties of Amsterdam and Tampere, remains in the Third Pillar of EU law, and is controlled by the national legislatures of member states, within the limits set by common EU guidelines and the Geneva Convention on the Status of Refugees (United Nations 1951).

(4) Since access to entry is still determined by individual states, the status of third-country nationals is subject to considerable variation across individual EU borders.

Rights of mobility, domicile, and employment are not union-wide. Article II-45 of the Treaty of the Constitution vaguely states that "Freedom of movement and residence may be granted, in accordance with the Constitution, to nationals of third countries legally resident in the territory of a Member State" (european-convention.eu.int/docs/Treaty/cv00820.en03.pdf).

(5) Throughout the EU a decoupling of national and cultural origin from the privileges of political membership is visible: European Union citizenship makes it possible to vote, run for, and hold office in local as well as union-wide elections for all EU citizens; this is not the case for third-country nationals. Their entitlement to political rights remains attached to their national and cultural origins. In this respect, too, changes are visible throughout the EU: in Denmark, Sweden, Finland, and the Netherlands third-country nationals can participate in local and regional elections; in Ireland these rights are granted at the local but not the regional levels. In the UK, Commonwealth citizens can vote in national elections as well.

(6) Tables 4.1 and 4.2 summarize the rights regimes to which different groups of individuals are subject.

Contemporary developments within the European Union reveal both the disaggregation of citizenship and the continuing problematic coupling of nationality with political privileges.[12] While throughout the EU a dissociation of

---

[12] Turks and ethnic Kurds (in most cases who are themselves Turkish citizens) are the largest group of foreigners not only in Germany, but in western Europe in general. In 1993, they numbered 2.7 million. Of that

the privileges of political citizenship from nationality can be observed for EU citizens, for third-country nationals, the ties between identities and institutions, between national membership and democratic citizenship rights, are reinforced. The dominant model is access to political rights through naturalization, i.e., through assuming the nationality of the host country. Most EU countries permit citizenship by naturalization (with the exception of Greece and Luxembourg); and, after the reform of Germany's *jus sanguinis* citizenship law in January 1999, most EU countries practice a form of more or less liberalized *jus soli*.

There are three competing models of political incorporation of immigrants into the European Union: the German, the French, and the Dutch. The German model favors nationalization through naturalization and the extension of political rights to third-country nationals as a result of their decision

number, 2.1 million live in Germany and as of 1999 make up 2.86 percent of the population. The second-largest group of foreigners are the members of former Yugoslav states, many of whom enjoy either full or temporary refugee status: 1.8 million Croats, Serbians, Bosnian Muslims, and Albanians. This picture is complicated by the presence in countries such as France of former colonials, such as the Algerians. As of the 1990 census, France counted 614,200 Algerian-born individuals among its population, and 572,200 Moroccans. In 1996 third-country national foreigners made up 6.3 percent of the population in France; in 1999 this percentage declined to 5.6 percent; and, according to the 2002 figures, it hovers around 6.1 percent. After the fall of communism in eastern and central Europe, migration from these countries to the EU has continued. In 1998, a total of 100,000 Polish citizens entered the EU. With the accession of Poland to the union in 2004, their status changed. In 1998, there were about 20,500 Russian citizens resident in Finland. See SOPEMI Publications 1998.

to forfeit the citizenship of their countries of origin. All children born to parents one of whom has been a legal resident in Germany for eight years automatically obtain German citizenship. At age twenty-three they must forfeit either German citizenship or that of the country of origin.

The French model, like the German one, accepts an equalization of the political-participation rights of third-country nationals only after they are naturalized. The French model is more liberal than the German one in that the granting of *jus soli* citizenship to immigrant children is not dependent on the residency status of their parents; their access to French citizenship is automatic once they have resided in France during their formative high-school years. Children born in France of two foreign-born parents are French if they live in France and have done so throughout adolescence. Immigrant children born on French soil become citizens at thirteen through the request of their parents, at sixteen through their own request, and automatically at eighteen.

The one exception to this trend toward "political participation through nationalization" is the Dutch model. This model is quite unique in that it grants city-citizenship to foreigners after five years of residency and permits them to take part in city-wide elections and to form political parties. The granting of political rights to third-country national residents in a city such as Amsterdam does not alter their status within the EU. They are still unable to move freely to other EU countries and to assume residence and employment there. But the fact that their interests and voices are represented at the municipal level means that they are more effective participants in the national dialogue concerning their juridical status than

Table 4.1 *Current rights regimes in contemporary Europe: civil and political rights*

Types of rights and entitlements	C (citizen)	EU R (resident)	EU T (temporary)	Third-country national, resident	Third-country national, temporary	Refugees and asylees (in process)
Human rights/civil rights *Protection of life, liberty, and property; due process of law (Article 6 of ECHR); rights of association in economy, civil society, and cultural life; freedom of speech and opinion (Article 11 of ECHR)*	**Full**	**Full**	**Full**	**Some restrictions** *Limited right of movement within EU states; limited rights of employment and contract; no rights of domicile other than in countries of residence; some constraints on political rights of association*	**Restricted**	**Restricted** *No rights of movement except as stipulated by host country; limited right to employment after 3 months* *Freedom of speech, opinion, and marriage; but no rights of political association* *Limited rights of appeal of decisions concerning asylum/refugee status*
Political rights *Run for, hold, and vote for office at all levels: local, regional, and national; establish political, civil, and cultural associations*	**Full**	**Partial** *No national voting rights; vote, run, stand for and hold office at local, regional, and EU elections after completion of residency*	**None**	**Limited** **Denmark, Finland, the Netherlands, Sweden** *grant local and regional election rights to foreigners who have fulfilled residency requirements;*	**None**	**None**

			Ireland, Italy grant local but not regional rights (Italy – legal, but not in effect); **Spain, Portugal** exercise reciprocity rights; **Dutch cities** grant city voting rights after 5 years; **UK** grants local and national voting rights to Commonwealth residents and citizens	None	None
Military service	Full	None	None	**Some** **France and Italy:** residents as well as asylees are draftable (no compulsory military service in Italy for those born after 1/1/1985)	None	None

Key: ECHR: European Convention for the Protection of Human Rights and Fundamental Freedoms.

R: An EU citizen resident in an EU country other than that of nationality for over 6 months; "permanent residency" granted after 5 years.

T: An EU citizen who is temporarily visiting, residing etc. in an EU country other than that of nationality.

Third-country national, resident: A third-country national who is residing in an EU country with an official residence permit.

Third-country national, temporary: A third-country national who is temporarily visiting or residing in an EU country.

Refugees and asylees (in process): Refugees and asylees whose applications are in the process of being considered and whose status is indeterminate.

Note and source: I would like to thank Willem Maas and Raluca Eddon for their help in compiling and preparing this information. I have greatly benefited from Guild 1996, 47–50.

Table 4.2 *Current rights regimes in contemporary Europe: social rights*

Social rights	C (citizen)	EU R (resident)	EU T (temporary)	Third-country national, resident	Third-country national, temporary	Refugees and asylees (in process)
Collective bargaining and trade unions	Full	Full	None or limited Students, for example	Full	None or limited Students, for example	None
Old age pensions	Full	Partial *(plan in country of origin and labor contract)*	None	Partial *Dependent on terms of employment contract between host and receiving country*	None *(country of origin)*	None
Unemployment benefits	Full	Partial	None	Partial *Dependent on labor contract; can lead to termination of residency permit, and non-renewal status*	None	None
Health care	Full	Full	Some *Students, for example*	Full	Some *Students, for example*	Some

Housing/child care/educational subsidies	Full	Full	Some — Students may be entitled to some benefits	Most — Subsidies for low-income family housing; education of children in own language in some cases; child care facilities	Some — Student housing; guest worker language courses and vocational schooling	Some — Free lodging; schooling of children
Cultural rights (schooling in own language, cultural and art subsidies)	Full	**National minority cultural regimes** (*if they exist at all*) — Some: Depends on size and history of resident non-nationals (instruction in own language may or may not be available; cultural and artistic subsidies would be)	Limited — Would have rights of EU residents	Currently contested; permits great national variation. **Germany, Netherlands** offer generous religious, language and cultural subsidies; **France** promotes cultural associations; **UK** does at local council levels, e.g., London	Limited — Share in rights of resident TCNs; if student for example	Some — Legal counsel and representation in own language (human right guaranteed by ECHR); schooling of children in home-country language may be available

Key: See key for table 4.1.

third-country residents of other EU countries are (see Tillie and Slijper forthcoming).

The existing discrepancy between the political-participation rights of EU citizens and third-country nationals *across* the EU, and *within* each member country, is one aspect of the two-tiered status of membership that is currently developing. Equally significant are the restrictions on the mobility and employment opportunities of third-country legal residents. Given the totally unclear status of European citizenship as distinct from national membership, EU-wide residency and citizenship rights for third-country nationals are still unavailable, though not inconceivable in principle.

The integration of third-country nationals into the civil and social rights regimes in EU countries is quite advanced, while the status of temporary residents, such as students or tourists visiting for personal, business, and professional reasons, is in line with international norms. There is some contention around the rights of political and civil association of temporary third-country residents. For example, can foreign students join unions? What kind of political organizations can they establish? While most EU countries actively encourage the development of civil, religious, and cultural associations, seeing in them steps toward more successful integration (Kastoryano 2002), political-association rights such as the establishment of political parties, lobbying groups, and student organizations are heavily monitored (and increasingly so since September 11, 2001).

What table 4.1 and table 4.2 also reveal is the extent to which refugees and asylum seekers are still denied the "right to have rights" in the full sense. While their life, liberty, and any property which they may have are protected by Article 6 of the European Convention on Human Rights and Fundamental Freedoms, their rights of movement, employment, and association are heavily curtailed. They are completely dependent upon the will of the sovereign state which grants them temporary sojourn. The transitory nature of their stay is accentuated even more by restrictions on their employment capacities. Often confined to segregated housing blocks in rural and urban centers, frequently cut off from the community around them, and denied the right to seek employment, refugees and asylum seekers become easy targets for xenophobic outbursts and sentiments. Nation-states retain them in a state of "exception" (Schmitt [1927] 1996, 47–49). They cannot appeal the decisions concerning their status and may raise no claims against deportation orders. Refugees and asylees are treated as if they were quasi-criminal elements, whose interaction with the larger society is to be closely monitored. They exist at the limits of all rights regimes and reveal the blind spot in the system of rights, where the rule of law flows into its opposite: the state of the exception and the ever-present danger of violence.

Identities and institutions: hopes and illusions of the new Europe

As the countries of Europe move together to forge a "an ever closer union among the peoples of Europe" (Treaty of Rome 1957), the traumas of the past, as well the dreams of the future, have created an unprecedented soul-searching. Remarkable discursive and geopolitical configurations have taken place on the old continent: some see the current condition as a return to the Roman Empire and the emergence of a new *pax romana*. Increasingly subject to a body of administrative law, able to enjoy the benefits and luxuries of civil and economic existence across Europe, today's EU citizens recall the ancient Romans, but not in their period of republican virtue. Rather, it is the Roman Empire, with its decadent and peaceful lifestyle and eclipsed republican political and martial skills that resonates with today's imagination. Those who invoke this memory often bemoan the disappearance of republican institutions of sovereignty and self-governance through the ordinances of an increasingly powerful Eurocracy (Guéhenno 1995).

Others argue that Europe is experiencing the resurgence of a "new medievalism" (Friedrichs 2001). The process of European integration has undermined the institutions of the nation-state and has empowered substate agencies and actors to gain new autonomy. The EU encourages regionalism and, in fact, subsidizes and provides incentives for regional European cooperation. Economic and political cooperation between Barcelona, Marseilles, and northern Italian towns such as Milan and Bologna is more extensive and intensive than the cooperation of these regions with other cities and regions in their own countries. Also, the principle of "subsidiarity," one of the cornerstones of new European governance, states that problems and issues are to be solved at the level of those most immediately affected by them (Article I-9, "Treaty Establishing a Constitution"). In many cases, subsidiarity encourages circumventing or avoiding the power of centralized national authorities. The "new medievalists" argue that regionalism, along with the principle of subsidiarity, generates structures of sovereignty which increasingly resemble the decentered, interlocked, and nested unities of medieval Europe. Unlike in the modern nation-state, there is no overlap any more between territoriality, authority, and sovereignty; rather, a functional system of authority has developed which is in turn integrated into supranational and extra-territorial unities.

Finally, there are those who regard these two preceding scenarios as fanciful constructs and who point out that Europe remains a Europe of nation-states and that the EU bears more resemblance to eighteenth-century dreams of a European federation governed by cosmopolitan ideals than to either the Roman Republic or the medieval past. The language of federalism and confederalism in which nation-states continue as discrete units with ultimate power of decision remains the guiding vision of the EU political elite and the bureaucracy. The drafting and adoption of the Treaty Establishing a Constitution for Europe has given "Euro-federalists" new hope and energy. The motto of the Constitutional Treaty, "united in diversity," cleverly leaves ambiguous whether it is the member-states or the peoples of Europe who are the source of this diversity. Clearly, the two are not identical, since there are non-state peoples in Europe such as the Basques, the Kurds, and the Gypsies, among others, who are not represented in the official organs of the EU.

Since the Copenhagen accords of 1993, conditions for admission to full membership have been defined very broadly to include (1) a demonstration of a country's commitment to functioning democratic institutions, human rights, the rule of law, and respect for and protection of minorities; (2) a competitive market economy as well as the capacity to cope with competitive pressure; and (3) evidence that the country is able to take on the obligations of membership, including adherence to the aims of political, economic, and monetary union. By focusing on such broad institutional criteria, the European Union hopes to avoid the much more controversial issues concerning cultural, linguistic, religious, and ethnic *identities*. The EU supposedly rests on a proven capacity to sustain a set of *institutions*, which, while originating in the West, are in principle capable of functioning on other soils and in other cultures as well. European identity is not given a thick cultural or historical coating; no exclusionary appeals are made to commonalties of history or faith, language or customs.

Despite these noble wishes to build the EU on "thin" liberal-democratic institutional criteria rather than on "thick" cultural identities, both within member states and at their borders, a deep conflict between institutional principles and identity has unfolded. The denial of Turkey's accession to membership talks in December 2003 and their postponement until 2004 became the occasion for a controversial debate about the Copenhagen criteria and EU's own cultural identity. Could the EU tolerate a Muslim-majority nation with a population of 65 million people in its midst? Unable to reach consensus around this issue, the European Council postponed the discussion (see Benhabib 2003).

As has often been the case in European history, xenophobic politics is easy politics, but the social factors and institutional trends behind immigration trends in contemporary Europe are much more complicated and intractable. Europe's "others," be they guest workers or refugees, asylum seekers or migrants, have become an obvious focus for the anxieties and uncertainties generated by Europe's own "othering," its transformation from a continent of nation-states into a transnational political entity, whose precise constitutional and political form is still uncertain. Nevertheless, as the institutional developments outlined above indicate, there is a dynamic toward narrowing the divide separating human rights from citizens' rights, or basic rights from political rights. The integration of third-country nationals into the EU's rights regime is well advanced and, given the growing role of the European Court of Justice and of the European Court of Human Rights, these trends are quite irreversible. Precisely because first entry sets into motion a trajectory toward full integration, it is likely that future policy in the EU will be to restrict access to borders more severely rather than dismantling the rights of resident foreigners.

The dialectic of rights and identities

This chapter began with a philosophical exploration of the justification of rights in a postmetaphysical universe. I argued that, if the practice of justification were to have any meaning at all, then the communicative freedom of individuals to engage in such justificatory practices ought to be presupposed. Rights, I maintained, could be viewed as the enabling preconditions of the exercise of communicative freedom, that is, of one's capacity to assent or to dissent from normative regulations through reasons. I distinguished further between the *principle of rights* and the *schedule of rights*. The latter, I maintained, could show democratic variations across countries and legislatures, depending on a myriad of factors.

Examining the evolution of a common rights regime within contemporary Europe, we see clearly that the greatest crossnational variations occur in the domain of social, economic, and cultural rights. While political rights are being reconfigured throughout the EU, human rights and civil rights are based on general rights instruments such as the UN Declaration of Human Rights and the European Convention for the Protection of Human Rights and Fundamental Freedoms. Human rights have acquired a fundamental, non-negotiable status; they are intended to be subject to the least variation on a country-by-country basis. They accrue to the human person because of his/her human dignity.

Nevertheless, and although great strides have been made since World War II in ameliorating the condition of stateless peoples, refugees, and asylum seekers, Hannah Arendt's observation that to lose one's citizenship status appeared tantamount to losing human rights altogether is not altogether wrong. Even in one of the most developed rights regimes of our world, refugees and asylum seekers still find themselves in quasi-criminal status. Their human rights are curtailed; they have no civil and political rights of association and representation. The extension of full human rights to these individuals and the decriminalization of their status is one of the most important tasks of cosmopolitan justice in our world.

These developments also suggest a dialectic of rights and identities: commonly, the individual who is the subject of rights is assumed to have some kind of fixed identity which precedes the entitlement to the right in question, but what is frequently neglected is that the exercise of rights themselves and the practice of political agency can change these identities. Political identities are endogenous and not exogenous to processes of democratic iteration and the formation of rights. Likewise, the meanings of rights claims are altered when exercised by subjects whose legal and political agency had not been foreseen or normatively anticipated in the initial formulations of rights. I would like to suggest that in the case of such dialectical conflicts we enter the domain of what Frank Michelman has called "jurisgenerative politics" (1988), namely contestation around rights and legal institutions which themselves pave the way for *new* modes of political agency and interaction. Contrary to decline-of-citizenship theorists, who see migrations as detrimental to a country's political and legal culture, the presence of individuals whose cultural identities differ from the majority introduces a dimension of "jurisgenerative politics" into the commonwealth. These are processes through which others become hermeneutical partners with us by reappropriating and reinterpreting our institutions and cultural traditions. The next chapter will assess the potentials of disaggregated citizenship and jurisgenerative politics.

5

Democratic iterations: the local, the national, and the global

Should we view the disaggregation of citizenship and the end of the unitary model with dismay? Are these developments indicators of the "devaluation" of citizenship, a trend toward "lean citizenship" (Thaa 2001), insofar as one no longer need be a citizen to have access to some coveted social rights? Or are these developments indicators of a new sense of global justice and harbingers of new modalities of political agency, heralding perhaps cosmopolitan citizenship?

This chapter begins by examining the ambivalences of disaggregated citizenship. Returning to the paradox of democratic legitimacy outlined in chapter 1, I argue that democratic rule has been based on various constitutive illusions such as the homogeneity of the people and territorial self-sufficiency. The challenge today is to reconfigure democratic voice without resorting to these illusions. To concretize what such a reconfiguration of democratic voice may entail, I discuss three cases of "jurisgenerative politics" in which challenges arising in interpreting "the rights of others" initiate self-reflexive transformations on the part of the polity involved.

The ambivalent potential of disaggregated citizenship

The European Union reproduces at the supranational level the internal tensions that have accompanied the birth of modern nation-states, while also showing their evolution along a different path. The modern nation-state fused together the culturally homogenizing and *identitarian* understandings of the citizenry with more democratic and pluralist variants, through processes of contestation, struggle, and cooperation as well as cooptation. T. H. Marshall focused on citizenship rights in the modern state in order to analyze how a capitalist state which rested on the sale of wage-labor through contract could nonetheless win the allegiance of the working classes by granting them a "status" – the status of citizenship. Marshall saw in these developments a reversal of Sir Henry Maine's well-known typology, "from status to contract," in that citizenship had to be considered a status whose value could not be affected adversely by the wage-labor contract. Citizenship remedied and rectified the indignities of capitalist inequality by giving the working classes access to the material conditions necessary for a "civilized existence" – a very important category in Marshall's essay.[1] Yet these compensatory achievements of citizenship status were dependent in crucial ways upon the presence of those who did not have access to citizenship and upon whom were heaped not only the indignities of wage-labor but those of being excluded from the commonwealth as well. Marshall could not admit, as Kant so blithely could, that they were "mere auxiliaries to the commonwealth" (Kant [1797] 1922, 121; [1797] 1996, 140). It is poignant in retrospect to read the naivete with which Marshall neglects the relationship of republic and empire, of

---

[1] "Status differences can receive the stamp of legitimacy in terms of democratic citizenship provided they do not cut too deep, *but occur within a population united in a single civilization*": Marshall 1950, 44; see also 47. My emphasis.

insiders and outsiders, and has nothing to say about the presence of those foreigners whose cheap labor in part subsidized the glories of the British welfare state.

I recall these insights and illusions of Marshall's renowned essay on "Citizenship and Social Class" because there is a widespread trend in contemporary political thought to look upon the formation of collective identities and the evolution of cultural solidarities not as having been attained through long, drawn-out, and bitter social and political conflicts, but as if they were stable givens. It is this static vision of collective-identity formation which makes it plausible for Michael Walzer, and following him John Rawls, to assume that aliens and others may pose a threat to, dilute, or overrun an already attained community of solidarity. The collective identities of liberal democracies have never been characterized by the degree of cohesiveness and culture-centeredness that these theorists attribute to them. To want to excise the outsiders or to close one's doors to newcomers is always accompanied by the need to discipline the outsiders within and to prevent reform, innovation, dissent, and transformation within the walls of one's own parish. The politics of immigration is closely linked to the politics of conformism and disciplining the opposition at home.

Trends toward the disaggregation of citizenship (see Ong 1999) are an inescapable aspect of contemporary globalization. But is disaggregated citizenship also democratic citizenship? Advocates of postnational citizenship welcome the uncoupling of political identities from national membership. James Rosenau (1997) and Yasemin Soysal (1994), for example, see the rise and spread of a new human rights regime, despite all its pitfalls and hypocrisies worldwide, as heralding a new political consciousness and new forms of political membership. The nation-state is waning; the line between human rights and citizens' rights is being corroded. New modalities of deterritorialized citizenship are emerging. Especially within the European Union, argues Soysal, national identities and allegiances are being scrambled rapidly, and it would be hypocritical to want to make "good Germans" out of Turks when contemporary Germans themselves are hardly sure what their own collective identity consists of (ibid.). Multicultural enclaves in large cities everywhere in the world are harbingers of the new faces of a citizenship which is no longer based upon exclusive attachments to a particular land, history, and tradition.

Surely, advocates of deterritorialized citizenship are correct that political identities need not be conceived exclusively in state-centric terms: the boundaries of the civic community and the boundaries of the state territory are not coterminous. Nonetheless, democratic commitment to a locality which may be smaller or larger than the nation-state is significant, and democratic governance implies drawing boundaries and creating rules of membership. The boundaries of communities of self-governance may not overlap with those of the nation-state, but the normative challenges of articulating boundaries will not simply disappear once we have made this observation.

Disaggregated citizenship permits individuals to develop and sustain multiple allegiances and networks across nation-state boundaries, in inter- as well as transnational contexts. Cosmopolitanism, the concern for the world as if it were one's *polis*, is furthered by such multiple, overlapping allegiances which are sustained across communities of language, ethnicity, religion, and nationality. Such networks are conducive to democratic citizenship if, and only if, they are accompanied by active involvement with and attachment to representative institutions, which exhibit accountability, transparency, and responsibility toward a given constituency that authorizes them in its own name. Transnational networks without democratic attachments can enhance fundamentalism as well as terrorism. It may be uncomfortable, but is nevertheless necessary, to recall that international terrorism is also a transnational phenomenon that manipulates and undermines existing nation-states.

At a deeper level, there is a tension between democratic legitimacy and the realities of disaggregated citizenship. Insofar as the self-constitution of "we, the people," is understood as if it were the unilateral act of a homogeneous citizenry, this idealized model of democratic legitimacy not only distorts historical facts, but cannot do justice to the normative potential of democratic constitutionalism. The human rights principles invoked by democratic constitutions have a context-transcending, cosmopolitan character. They extend to all of humankind. Their territorial delimitation involves war as well as conquest, negotiation as well as bargaining. The democratic people constitutes itself as sovereign over a territory only through such historically contingent processes, and these attest to the violence inherent in every act of self-constitution.

If we focus on the cosmopolitan content of rights claims and on the principle of democratic voice, we need to move toward a vision of reflexive acts of constitution-making which are cognizant of the fact that political entities act in an environment crowded with other political actors, and that acts of self-constitution are not unilateral gestures – although very often they have been understood to be just that. Policies governing immigration, refuge, and asylum are affected by other political entities. As Max Pensky points out: "All modern constitutions offer membership according to a schedule of rights, and these rights are justified in terms of universal, rather than merely local or parochial, attributes of members . . . Modern constitutions therefore tend to make normative claims that they cannot possibly fulfill. This is one way of describing the problem of constitutional scope. The normative force of democratic constitutions coherently demands the extension of inclusion to all persons while simultaneously retracting that inclusion to all members of a set of arbitrarily designated persons in order to actually succeed in *constituting* a polity" (Pensky 2002; emphasis in the text). The evolution of disaggregated citizenship has the virtue of making all too apparent the internal tensions of democratic constitutions. Aware of the cosmopolitan potential of rights, which transcended historically contingent political borders, Kant therefore argued that a republican constitution, one that would not be based on simple majority rule, would lead toward a federation of world republics (see ch. 1).

Democratic iterations and jurisgenerative politics

The position which I have characterized as cosmopolitan federalism suggests that, between the norms of international law and the actions of individual democratic legislatures, multiple "iterations" are possible and desirable. The two are

not mutually exclusive. Cosmopolitan norms today are becoming embedded in the political and legal culture of individual polities. Transformations of citizenship, through which
rights are extended to individuals by virtue of residency rather
than cultural identity, are the clearest indicators of such cosmopolitan norms. Nonetheless, and insofar as those whose
membership status remains unresolved – such as undocumented migrants, refugees, and asylees whose applications are
in process – are treated as if they were criminals by existing
polities, cosmopolitanism in the international arena has not
been attained. The right to universal hospitality is sacrificed
on the altar of state interest. We need to decriminalize the
worldwide movement of peoples, and treat each person, whatever his or her political citizenship status, in accordance with
the dignity of moral personhood. This implies acknowledging
that crossing borders and seeking entry into different polities is not a criminal act but an expression of human freedom
and the search for human betterment in a world which we
have to share with our fellow human beings. First admittance
does not imply automatic membership. Democratic peoples
will still have to devise rules of membership at the national,
subnational, regional, and municipal levels. It is the people
themselves who, through legislation and discursive will- and
opinion-formation, must adopt policies and laws consonant
with the cosmopolitan norms of universal hospitality. Defining the identity of the democratic people is an ongoing process
of constitutional self-creation. While we can never eliminate
the paradox that those who are excluded will not be among
those who decide upon the rules of exclusion and inclusion, we can render these distinctions fluid and negotiable

through processes of continuous and multiple democratic iterations.

The treatment of aliens, foreigners, and others in our midst is a crucial test case for the moral conscience as well as political reflexivity of liberal democracies. Defining the identity of the sovereign nation is itself a process of fluid, open, and contentious public debate: the lines separating we and you, us and them, more often than not rest on unexamined prejudices, ancient battles, historical injustices, and sheer administrative fiat. The beginnings of every modern nation-state carry the seeds of some violence and injustice; in that, Carl Schmitt is right ([1923] 1985). Nonetheless, modern liberal democracies are self-limiting collectivities which, at one and the same time, constitute the *demos* as sovereign while proclaiming that the sovereignty of this *demos* derives its legitimacy from its adherence to fundamental human rights principles. "We, the people," is an inherently fraught formula, containing in its very articulation the constitutive dilemmas of respect for universal human rights and nationally circumscribed sovereignty claims. The rights of foreigners and aliens, whether they be refugees or guest workers, asylum seekers or adventurers, define that threshold, that boundary, at the site of which the identity of "we, the people," is defined and renegotiated, bounded and unraveled, circumscribed and rendered fluid. We are at a point in political evolution when the unitary model of citizenship, which bundled together residency upon a single territory with the subjection to a single administration of a people perceived to be a more or less cohesive entity, is at an end. The end of this model does not mean that its hold upon our political imagination and its normative force in guiding our institutions are obsolete. It does mean that we must be ready to imagine forms of political agency and subjectivity which anticipate new modalities of political citizenship. I want to characterize these new political trends through the concept of "democratic iterations."

By *democratic iterations* I mean complex processes of public argument, deliberation, and exchange through which universalist rights claims and principles are contested and contextualized, invoked and revoked, posited and positioned, throughout legal and political institutions, as well as in the associations of civil society. These can take place in the "strong" public bodies of legislatures, the judiciary, and the executive, as well as in the informal and "weak" publics of civil society associations and the media.

Iteration is a term which was introduced into the philosophy of language through Jacques Derrida's work ([1982] 1991, 90ff.). In the process of repeating a term or a concept, we never simply produce a replica of the first original usage and its intended meaning: rather every repetition is a form of variation. Every iteration transforms meaning, adds to it, enriches it in ever-so-subtle ways. In fact, there really is no "originary" source of meaning, or an "original" to which all subsequent forms must conform. It is obvious in the case of language that an act of original meaning-giving makes no sense, since, as Wittgenstein famously reminded us, to recognize an act of meaning-giving as such an act, we would already need to possess language itself (Wittgenstein, 1953) – a patently circular notion!

Nevertheless, even if the concept of "original meaning" makes no sense when applied to language as such, it may not be so ill placed in conjunction with documents such as the law and institutional norms. Thus, every act of iteration might refer to an antecedent which is taken to be authoritative. The iteration and interpretation of norms, and of every aspect of the universe of value, however, are never merely acts of repetition. Every act of iteration involves making sense of an authoritative original in a new and different context. The antecedent thereby is repositioned and resignified via subsequent usages and references. Meaning is enhanced and transformed; conversely, when the creative appropriation of that authoritative original ceases or stops making sense, then the original loses its authority upon us as well. Iteration is the reappropriation of the "origin"; it is at the same time its dissolution as the original and its preservation through its continuous deployment.

Democratic iterations are such linguistic, legal, cultural, and political repetitions-in-transformation, invocations which are also revocations. They not only change established understandings but also transform what passes as the valid or established view of an authoritative precedent. Robert Cover (1983), and following him Frank Michelman (1988),[2]

---

[2] "The conclusion emanating from this state of affairs," writes Robert Cover, "is simple and very disturbing: there is a radical dichotomy between the social organization of law as power and the organization of law as meaning. This dichotomy, manifest in folk and underground cultures in even the most authoritarian societies, is particularly open to view in a liberal society that disclaims control over narrative. The uncontrolled character of meaning exercises a destabilizing influence upon power. Precepts must 'have meaning,' but they necessarily borrow it from materials created by social activity that is not subject to the strictures of provenance that characterize what we call formal lawmaking. Even when authoritative institutions try to create meaning for the precepts they articulate, they act, in that respect, in an unprivileged fashion" (1983, 18).

have made these observations fruitful in the domain of legal interpretation. *Jurisgenerative politics* refers to iterative acts through which a democratic people that considers itself bound by certain guiding norms and principles reappropriates and reinterprets these, thus showing itself to be not only the *subject* but also the *author of the laws.* Whereas natural right doctrines assume that the principles that undergird democratic politics are impervious to transformative acts of will, and whereas legal positivism identifies democratic legitimacy with the correctly posited norms of a sovereign legislature, jurisgenerative politics signals a space of interpretation and intervention between transcendent norms and the will of democratic majorities. The rights claims which frame democratic politics, on the one hand, must be viewed as transcending the specific enactments of democratic majorities under specific circumstances; on the other hand, such democratic majorities *re-iterate* these principles and incorporate them into democratic will-formation processes through argument, contestation, revision, and rejection.

In the following I focus on three complex legal, political, and cultural phenomena through which democratic iterations have occurred and collective resignifications have emerged: I begin with the so-called scarf affair, or *l'affaire du foulard,* which has preoccupied French public opinion and politics throughout the 1990s. The banning of the wearing of the headscarf by Muslim girls in schools pitted the right to freedom of conscience, to which all French citizens and residents alike are entitled, against the specific French understanding of the separation of church and state, known as the principle of *laïcité.* This affair led to a debate, which is still continuing, about the meaning of French citizenship for an increasingly multicultural and multifaith society. The extension of a democratic schedule of rights to citizens and residents alike in a member country of the European Union, such as France is, brings in its wake controversy about who precisely the subject of rights is. Can an observant Muslim woman be a good French citizen and also be true to herself? And what exactly does it mean to be a "good" French citizen? Who defines the terms here?

Much like France, contemporary Germany as well is by now a multicultural and multifaith society, with a resident foreign population approximating 10 percent of the total. Among these foreigners, those of Muslim faith, such as the Turks, Kurds, Pakistanis, Afghanis, and others, constitute the majority. Confronted with a case much like the *affaire du foulard* in France, recently the German Supreme Court tried to take a middle line by upholding in principle the freedom of conscience of a Muslim schoolteacher to teach with her head covered, yet transferred the ultimate decision in the case to the will of the democratic sovereign.

Unlike France, Germany until recently had not accepted naturalization of immigrant children through territorial birthright. The German understanding of citizenship has been less expansive and republican than the French one, and has focused much more on ethnic belonging. However, this antiquated understanding of German citizenship could hardly be reconciled with the realities of modern Germany as a regional and global economic superpower. One of the first challenges to the restrictive German understanding of citizenship came as a request from the city-states of Hamburg and the province of Schleswig-Holstein to permit non-citizen but long-term resident foreigners to vote in municipal and district elections. The German Constitutional Court rejected their request through a resounding excursus on the role of the nation and national belonging in a democracy. Although the Maastricht Treaty (1993), to which Germany is a party, has since then overridden this decision by granting all nationals of EU member states who are residents of other member countries the right to vote in and run for municipal elections, the earlier decision remains one of the most philosophically interesting interpretations of the democratic sovereignty as emanating from a culturally and ethnically homogeneous people.

L'affaire du foulard (the scarf affair)

A consequence of the transformation of citizenship is the long- and short-term coexistence of individuals and groups of distinct and often quite contradictory cultures, mores, and norms, in the same public space.[3] If globalization brings with it the ever-more rapid movement of peoples and goods, information and fashion, germs and news, across state boundaries, one consequence of these trends is their multidirectionality. Globalization does not simply mean the spread of multinational, and usually American, British, or Japanese-run, corporations around the globe. Benjamin

---

[3] Parts of this discussion have previously appeared in Benhabib 2002a, 94–100. I have revised the concluding sections in particular.

Barber's phrase "Jihad vs. McWorld" certainly captures a partial truth (Barber 1995). There is also the phenomenon of "reverse globalization," through which the peoples of the poorer regions of the world hailing from the Middle East, Africa, and Southeast Asia flock to global cities, such as London and Paris, Toronto and Rome, Madrid and Amsterdam. These groups, a good number of whom originally came to western countries as guest workers and immigrants, have seen their numbers multiply in the last decades through the entry of refugees and asylum seekers from other regions of the world. The most spectacular examples of multicultural conflict which have occupied public consciousness in recent decades, such as the Salman Rushdie affair in Great Britain, the affair over the *foulard* (headscarf) in French schools, and scandals around the practice of female circumcision, have concerned these new ethnocultural groups, as they have sought to adapt their religious and cultural beliefs to the legal and cultural environment of secular, but mostly Protestant, Catholic, or Anglican, liberal-democratic states.

On February 10, 2004, the French National Assembly voted by an overwhelming majority (494 for, 36 against, and 31 abstentions) to ban the wearing of all religious symbols from public schools. Although the new law applies to any ostentatiously displayed religious symbol such as Christian crosses and the yarmulkes of Orthodox Jewish student, as well as the headscarves worn by Muslim girls, its main target was Muslim religious attire. To understand the severity of this legislation, which drew criticism even from France's allies in the European Union, such as the British and the Dutch governments, it is important to reconstruct the history of the scarf affair.

L'affair du foulard[4] refers to a long and drawn-out set of public confrontations which began in France in 1989 with the expulsions from their school in Creil (Oise) of three scarf-wearing Muslim girls and continued to the mass exclusion of twenty-three Muslim girls from their schools in November 1996 upon the decision of the Conseil d'Etat.[5] The affair, referred to as a "national drama" (Gaspard and Kheosrokhavar 1995, 11)

[4] A note of terminological clarification first: the practice of veiling among Muslim women is a complex institution that exhibits great variety across many Muslim countries. The terms *chador, hijab, niqab,* and *foulard* refer to distinct items of clothing which are worn by Muslim women coming from different Muslim communities: for example, the *chador* is essentially Iranian and refers to the long black robe and headscarf worn in a rectangular manner around the face; the *niqab* is a veil that covers the eyes and the mouth and only leaves the nose exposed; it may or may not be worn in conjunction with the *chador.* Most Muslim women from Turkey are likely to wear either long overcoats and a *foulard* (a headscarf) or a *carsaf* (a black garment which most resembles the *chador*). These items of clothing have a symbolic function within the Muslim community itself: women coming from different countries signal to one another their ethnic and national origins through their clothing, as well as signifying their distance or proximity to tradition in doing so. The brighter the colors of their overcoats and scarves – bright blue, green, beige, or lilac as opposed to brown, grey, navy, and, of course, black – and the more fashionable their cuts and material by western standards, the more can we assume the distance from Islamic orthodoxy of the women who wear them. Seen from the outside, however, this complex semiotic of dress codes gets reduced to one or two items of clothing which then assume the function of crucial symbols in complex negotiations between Muslim communities and western cultures.

[5] My discussion of these incidents relies primarily upon two sources: Gaspard and Khosrokhavar 1995, and an excellent paper by Marianne Brun-Rovet, submitted to my seminar on "Nations, States, and Citizens," Harvard University, Department of Government Brun-Rovet (2000), on file with the author.

or even a "national trauma" (Brun-Rovet 2000, 2), occurred in the wake of France's celebration of the second centennial of the French Revolution and seemed to question the foundations of the French educational system and its philosophical principle, *laïcité*. This concept is hard to translate in terms like the "separation of church and state" or even secularization: at its best, it can be understood as the public and manifest neutrality of the state toward all kinds of religious practices, institutionalized through a vigilant removal of sectarian religious symbols, signs, icons, and items of clothing from official public spheres. Yet within the French Republic the balance between respecting the individual's right to freedom of conscience and religion, on the one hand, and maintaining a public sphere devoid of all religious symbolisms, on the other, was so fragile that it only took the actions of a handful of teenagers to expose this fragility. The ensuing debate went far beyond the original dispute and touched upon the self-understanding of French republicanism for the left as well as the right, on the meaning of social and sexual equality, and liberalism vs. republicanism vs. multiculturalism in French life.

The affair began when on October 19, 1989, M. Ernest Chenière, headmaster of the Collège Gabriel Havez of Creil, forbade three girls – Fatima, Leila, and Samira – to attend classes with their heads covered. The three had appeared in class that morning wearing their scarves, despite a compromise reached between their headmasters and their parents encouraging them to go unscarfed. The three girls had apparently decided to wear the scarf once more upon the advice of M. Daniel Youssouf Leclerq, the head of an organization called Intégrité and the ex-president of the National Federation of

Muslims in France. Although hardly noted in the press, the fact that the girls had been in touch with M. Leclerq indicates that wearing the scarf was a conscious political gesture on their part, a complex act of identification and defiance. In doing so, Fatima, Leila, and Samira on the one hand claimed to exercise their freedom of religion as French citizens; on the other hand, they exhibited their Muslim and North African origins in a context that sought to envelop them within an egalitarian, secularist ideal of republican citizenship as students of the nation. In the years to come, the girls and their followers and supporters forced what the French state wanted to view as a private symbol – an individual item of clothing – into the shared public sphere, thus challenging the boundaries between the public and the private. Ironically, they used the freedom given to them by French society and French political traditions, not the least of which is the availability of free and compulsory public education for all children on French soil, to transpose an aspect of their private identity into the public sphere. In doing so, they problematized the school as well as the home: they no longer treated the school as a neutral space of French acculturation but brought their cultural and religious differences into open manifestation. They used the symbol of the home to gain entry into the public sphere by retaining the modesty required of them by Islam in covering their heads; yet at the same time, they left the home to become public actors in a civil public space in which they defied the state. Those who saw in the girls' actions simply an indication of their oppression were just as blind to the symbolic meaning of their deeds as those who defended their rights simply on the basis of freedom of religion.

187

The French sociologists Gaspard and Khosrokhavar capture this set of complex symbolic negotiations as follows: "[The veil] mirrors in the eyes of the parents and the grandparents the illusions of continuity whereas it is a factor of discontinuity; it makes possible the transition to otherness (modernity), under the pretext of identity (tradition); it creates the sentiment of identity with the society of origin whereas its meaning is inscribed within the dynamic of relations with the receiving society ... it is the vehicle of the passage to modernity within a promiscuity which confounds traditional distinctions, of an access to the public sphere which was forbidden to traditional women as a space of action and the constitution of individual autonomy" (1995, 44–45. My translation).

The complexity of the social and cultural negotiations hidden behind the simple act of veiling elicited an equally ambiguous and complex decision by the French Conseil d'Etat (the French Supreme Court). On November 4, 1989, the then French minister of education, Lionel Jospin, took the matter to the Conseil d'Etat. The Conseil responded by citing France's adherence to constitutional and legislative texts and to international conventions, and invoked from the outset the necessity of doing justice to two principles: that the *laïcité* and neutrality of the state be retained in the rendering of public services and that the liberty of conscience of the students be respected. All discrimination based upon the religious convictions or beliefs of the students would be inadmissible. The Conseil then concluded that "the wearing by students, in the schools, of signs whereby they believe to be manifesting their adherence to one religion is itself not incompatible with the principle of *laïcité*, since it constitutes the exercise of their liberty of expression and manifestation of their religious beliefs; but this liberty does not permit students to exhibit [*d'arborer*] signs of religious belonging which, by their nature, by the conditions under which they are worn individually or collectively, or by their ostentatious or combative [*revindicatif*] character, would constitute an act of pressure, provocation, proselytizing, or propaganda, threatening to the dignity or liberty of the student or to the other members of the educational community, compromising their health or their security, disturbing the continuation of instructional activities or the educational role of the instructors, in short, which would disturb proper order in the establishment or the normal functioning of public service" (Ruling of the Conseil d'Etat of November 27, 1989. My translation).[6]

This Solomonic judgment attempted to balance the principles of *laïcité* and freedom of religion and conscience. Yet instead of articulating some clear guidelines, the Conseil left the proper interpretation of the meaning of wearing of such religious symbols and attire up to the judgment of the school authorities. Not the individual students' own beliefs about what a religious scarf (or for that matter yarmulke) meant to them but its interpretation by the school authorities and whether or not they could be seen as signs of provocation, confrontation, or remonstration became the decisive factors in curtailing the students' freedom of religion. It is not difficult to see why this judgment encouraged both sides in the conflict to pursue their goals further and led to further repression through the promulgation on September 10, 1994, of the Bayrou Guidelines, issued by Minister of Education François Bayrou. Lamenting

---

[6] Unless otherwise noted, translations in this chapter are mine.

the ambiguities of the judgment of the Conseil for conveying an impression of weaknesses vis-à-vis Islamist movements, the minister declared that students had the right to wear discreet religious symbols, but that the veil was not among them (*Le Monde*, September 12, 1994, 10).

L'affair du foulard eventually came to stand for all dilemmas of French national identity in the age of globalization and multiculturalism: how to retain French traditions of *laïcité*, republican equality, and democratic citizenship in view of France's integration into the European Union on the one hand, and the pressures of multiculturalism generated through the presence of second- and third-generation immigrants from Muslim countries on French soil on the other. Would the practices and institutions of French citizenship be flexible and generous enough to encompass multicultural differences within an ideal of republican equality? Clearly, this affair is by no means over and as European integration and multiculturalist pressures continue, France will have to discover new models of legal, pedagogical, social, and cultural institutions to deal with the dual imperatives of liberal democracies to preserve freedom of religious expression and the principles of secularism.

We seem to have a paradoxical situation here, in which the French state intervenes *to dictate* more autonomy and egalitarianism in the public sphere than the girls themselves wearing headscarves seem to wish for. What exactly is the meaning of the girls' actions? Is this an act of religious observance and subversion, or one of cultural defiance, or of adolescent acting out to gain attention and prominence? Are the girls acting out of fear, out of conviction, or out of narcissism? It is not hard to imagine that their actions may involve all these elements and motives. The girls' voices are not heard in this heated debate; although there was a genuine public discourse in the French public sphere and a soul-searching on the questions of democracy and difference in a multicultural society, as the sociologists Gaspard and Khosrokhavar pointed out, until they carried out their interviews (1995), the girls' own perspectives were hardly listened to. Even if the girls involved were not adults in the eyes of the law and were still under the tutelage of their families, it is reasonable to assume that at the ages of fifteen and sixteen, they could account for themselves and their actions. Had their voices been heard and listened to, it would have become clear that the meaning of wearing the scarf itself was changing from being a religious act to one of cultural defiance and increasing politicization (but see Giraud and Sintomer 2004). Ironically, it was the very egalitarian norms of the French public educational system that brought these girls out of the patriarchal structures of the home and into the French public sphere, and gave them the confidence and the ability to *resignify the wearing of the scarf.* Instead of penalizing and criminalizing their activities, would it not have been more plausible to ask these girls to account for their actions and doings at least to their school communities, and to encourage discourses among the youth about what it means to be a Muslim citizen in a *laic* French Republic? Unfortunately, the voices of those whose interests were most vitally affected by the norms prohibiting the wearing of the scarf under certain conditions were ignored.

I am not suggesting that legal norms should originate through collective discursive processes and outside the framework of legal institutions: the legitimacy of the law is not at stake in this example; rather it is the *democratic legitimacy* of a lawful but in my view unwise and unfair decision which is at stake. It would have been both more democratic and fairer if the meaning of their act was not simply dictated to these girls by their school authorities, and if they were given more of a public say in the interpretation of their own actions. Would or should this have changed the Conseil d'Etat's decision? Maybe not, but the clause which permitted the prohibition of "ostentatiously" and "demonstratively" displayed religious symbols should have been reconsidered. There is sufficient evidence in the sociological literature that in many other parts of the world as well Muslim women are using the veil as well as the *chador* to cover up the paradoxes of their own emancipation from tradition (see Göle 1996). To assume that the meaning of their actions is purely one of religious defiance of the secular state constrains these women's own capacity to write the meaning of their own actions and, ironically, reimprisons them within the walls of patriarchal meaning from which they are trying to escape.

Learning processes would have to take place on the part of the Muslim girls as well: while the larger French society would have to learn not to stigmatize and stereotype as "backward and oppressed creatures" all those who accept the wearing of what appears at first glance to be a religiously mandated piece of clothing, the girls themselves and their supporters, in the Muslim community and elsewhere, have to learn to give a justification of their actions with "good reasons in the public sphere." In claiming respect and equal treatment for their religious beliefs, they have to clarify how they intend to treat the beliefs of *others* from different religions, and how, in effect, they would institutionalize the separation of religion and the state within Islamic tradition.

There are some indications that, despite the harshness of recent events and confrontations between religious Islamic groups and the authorities, a moderate French Islam is emerging. On April 14, 2003, the *New York Times* reported the formation of an official Muslim Council to represent the 5 million Muslims of France. Among other issues, the council will deal with the rights of Muslim women in the workplace. Thus, Karima Debza, an Algerian-born mother of three, is reported as saying: "I cannot find work here because of my headscarf . . . But my headscarf is part of me. I won't take it off. We have to educate the state about why the scarf is so important," and she added, "and why there should be no fear of it" (Sciolino 2003a).

What Debza is asking for is a process of democratic iteration and cultural resignification. While she is urging her French cocitizens to reconsider the strict doctrine of *laïcisme*, which precludes her from appearing in public places with a symbol which bears religious meaning – i.e., the headscarf – she herself is resignifying the wearing of the scarf in terms which involve what some have called a "Protestantization" of Islam. The covering of one's head, which in Islam as well as Judaism is an aspect of women's modesty and also, more darkly, an aspect of the repression of female sexuality that is viewed as threatening, is now reinterpreted as a private act of faith and conscience. But in presenting the wearing of the scarf as an aspect of her identity and her self-understanding as a Muslim, Debza is transforming these traditional connotations and is pleading for reciprocal recognition from others of her right to wear the scarf, so long as doing so does not infringe upon the rights of others. "Because my wearing the scarf," Debza is saying, "is so fundamental to who I am" (her own words are "it is a part of me"), "you should respect it as long as it does not infringe on your rights and liberties." The wearing of the scarf is resignified as an act of conscience and as the expression of one's moral freedom. Her point can be summarized thus: the protection of the equal right to religious freedom of all citizens and residents of France (a right also protected by the European Convention for the Protection of Human Rights and Fundamental Freedoms) should be considered more fundamental – in Ronald Dworkin's terms should "trump" – the clause concerning the specific separation of religion and state which France practices – namely *laïcisme*. In this process, Debza states, "we have to educate the state not to fear us" – a marvelous thought coming from an immigrant Muslim woman vis-à-vis the daunting traditions of French republicanism.

The challenge posed to French traditions of *laïcité* should not be underestimated. The clause of the separation of religion and state, while being a cornerstone of liberal democracies, also permits significant democratic variation. Thus England has a Church of England, while Germany subsidizes the three officially recognized denominations – Protestant, Catholic, and Jewish – through an indirect "church tax" known as *Kirchensteuer*. Emerging out of the historical experience of anti-clericalism and antagonism toward the institutions of the Catholic Church, the French republican tradition finds itself faced today with a new challenge: how to accommodate demands for religious diversity in the context of global trends toward increasingly multicultural societies. Is the republican public sphere, cherished by French traditions, really defaced when individuals of different races, colors, and faiths want to function in this very public sphere carrying the signs and symbols of their private faiths and identities? Should their self-presentation through their particular identities be viewed as a threat to French understandings of citizenship?

Undoubtedly, after the events of September 11 and the Second Iraq War, the French government needs to retain the loyalty and civility of its 5 million Muslims rather than reenact the experiences of the revolutionary "republic of virtue." *Pace* Robespierre – the realities of multicultural coexistence require the transition from the republic of virtue to that of liberal civility.

In an explicit acknowledgment of the "changing face of France," both in the literal and figurative senses, during August 2003, thirteen women, eight of them of North African Muslim origin and the rest African immigrants or the children of immigrants, were chosen to represent "Marianne," the icon of the Revolution, painted in 1830 by Eugene Delacroix, bare-chested and storming the barricades. Continuing the contentious national dialogue about the separation of church and state, these women wore the ancient Phrygian cap, a symbol of the French Revolution, rather than the Islamic veil or other ethnic or national head-dress (Sciolino 2003b). Yet paradoxically, the political body that has decided to honor these women as a countersymbol to others like Debza who insist upon wearing the headscarf has also empowered these women to challenge the overwhelmingly white, male, and middle-aged French assembly, in which only 12 percent are women (ibid.). One of the women is quoted as saying: "These Mariannes have made visible something that has been the reality of the last twenty years. Look at the National Assembly. It's all white, rich, male, and well-educated. Now we have entered their space. We exist" (ibid.).[7]

Culture matters; cultural evaluations are deeply bound up with interpretations of our needs, our visions of the good life, and our dreams for the future. Since these evaluations run so deep, as citizens of liberal-democratic polities, we have to learn to live with what Michael Walzer has called "liberalism and the art of separation" (Walzer 1984). We have to learn to live with the otherness of others whose ways of being may be deeply threatening to our own. How else can moral and political learning take place, except through such encounters in civil society? The law provides the framework within which the work of culture and politics go on. The laws, as the ancients knew, are the walls of the city, but the art and passions of politics occur within those walls (see Arendt 1961) and very often politics leads to the breaking-down of these barriers or at least to assuring their permeability.

There is a dialectic between constitutional essentials and the actual politics of political liberalism. Rights, and other principles of the liberal democratic state, need to be periodically challenged and rearticulated in the public sphere in order

7 The severity of the law passed by the French National Assembly on February 10, 2004, banning the wearing of the scarf and other religious symbols in public schools will make the emergence of a moderate Islam much more difficult. But processes of democratic iteration will continue, as many French women's groups and even teachers' organizations question the wisdom of this legislation. Without a doubt, human rights groups as well as Muslim organizations will also challenge this law at the level of European courts. See " Derrière la voile" 2001.

to enrich their original meaning. It is only when new groups claim that they belong within the circles of addressees of a right from which they have been excluded in its initial articulation that we come to understand the fundamental limitedness of every rights claim within a constitutional tradition as well as its context-transcending validity. The democratic dialogue and also the legal hermeneutic one are enhanced through the repositioning and rearticulation of rights in the public spheres of liberal democracies. The law sometimes can guide this process, in that legal reform may run ahead of popular consciousness and may raise popular consciousness to the level of the constitution; the law may also lag behind popular consciousness and may need to be prodded along to adjust itself to it. In a vibrant liberal multicultural democracy, cultural-political conflict and learning through conflict should not be stifled through legal maneuvers. The democratic citizens themselves have to learn the art of separation by testing the limits of their overlapping consensus.

While the intervention of French authorities to ban the wearing of the veil in the schools at first seemed like the attempt of a progressive state bureaucracy to modernize the "backward-looking" customs of a group, this intervention cascaded into a series of democratic iterations. These ranged from the intense debate among the French public about the meaning of wearing the veil, to the self-defense of the girls involved and the rearticulation of the meaning of their actions, to the encouragement of other immigrant women to wear their headscarf into the work place, and, finally, to the very public act of resignifying the face of "Marianne," via having immigrant women from Arab as well as African countries represent it.

I do not want to underestimate, however, the extent of public dissatisfaction with and also significant xenophobic resentment toward France's Muslim population. Democratic iterations can lead to processes of public self-reflection as well generating public defensiveness. The mobilization of many right-wing parties throughout Europe is intensifying: in France, the Netherlands, the UK, Denmark, Germany, and elsewhere, we see well that the status of Europe's migrants and particularly of its Muslim population, especially after September 11, 2001, and the Madrid train station bombings in March 2004, remain incendiary issues. No matter how such political contentions may be resolved eventually, it is clear that they will be fought out within a framework created by the universalistic principles and intent of Europe's commitment to human rights on the one hand and the exigencies of democratic self-determination on the other.

The German scarf affair: the case of Fereshta Ludin

In recent years, the German public and the courts have dealt with a challenge quite akin to the scarf affair in France. An elementary schoolteacher in Baden-Württemberg, Fereshta Ludin, of Afghani origin and German citizenship, insisted on being able to teach her classes with her head covered (see Emcke 2000, 280–285). The school authorities refused to permit her to do so. The case ascended all the way to the German Constitutional Court (BVerfG) and on September 30, 2003, the court decided as follows. Wearing a headscarf, in the context presented to the court, expresses that the claimant belongs to the

"Muslim community of faith" (*die islamische Religionsgemein-schaft*). The court concluded that to describe such behavior as demonstrating a lack of qualification (*Eignungsmangel*) for the position of a teacher in elementary and middle schools clashed with the right of the claimant to equal access to all public offices in accordance with article 33, paragraph 2 of the Basic Law (*Grundgesetz*), and also clashed with her right to freedom of conscience, as protected by article 4, paragraphs 1 and 2 of the Basic Law, without, however, providing the required and sufficient lawful reasons for doing so (BVerfG, 2BvR, 1436/02, IVB 1 and 2). While acknowledging the fundamental rights of Fereshta Ludin, the court nevertheless rejected her plea and transferred the final say on the matter to the democratic legislatures. "The responsible provincial legislature is nevertheless free to create the legal basis [to refuse to permit her to teach with her head covered] by determining anew within the framework set by the constitution the extent of religious articles to be permitted in the schools. In this process, the provincial legislature must take into consideration the freedom of conscience of the teacher as well as of the students involved, and also the right to educate their children on the part of parents as well as the obligation of the state to retain neutrality in matters of worldview and religion" (BVerfG, 2BvR, 1436/02, 6).

While acknowledging the fundamental nature of the rights involved – those of freedom of conscience and equal access of all to public offices – the German Constitutional Court, much like the French Conseil d'Etat, refused to protect these against the will of the democratic legislatures. Yet by not leaving the case up to the exclusive jurisdiction of the school authorities, and by stressing the necessity for the state

THE RIGHTS OF OTHERS

to maintain religious and worldview neutrality in the matter, it signaled to democratic lawmakers the importance of respecting the legitimate pluralism of worldviews in a liberal democracy. Nevertheless, the court did not see itself justified in positively intervening to shield such pluralism, but considered this to fall into the domain of provincial legislation.[8] Such reticence may surprise some; undoubtedly, the fact that teachers in Germany are also *Beamten*, i.e., civil servants of the state who stand under the special jurisdiction of various civil service acts, may have played a role in the German Constitutional Court's not wanting to intervene in the regulatory jurisdiction of legislators. Nevertheless, it is hard to avoid the impression that the real worry of the court was more the substantive rather than the procedural question, as to whether a woman who ostensibly wore an object representing her belonging to "the traditions of her community of origin" could carry out the duties and tasks of a functionary of the German state.[9]

Despite the fact that Ludin was a German citizen of Afghani origin who had successfully completed the requisite qualifications to become a teacher according to German law, the cultural and religious significance of her wearing the scarf clashed with widely held beliefs about the public face of a teacher in German society. The two dimensions of her

---

[8] The German legislators responded to the mandate of the court rather speedily and, after Baden-Württemberg, Bavaria as well passed a bill banning the wearing of headscarves in schools. Christian and Jewish symbols were not included in this ban. Civil rights organizations and groups representing Muslims living in Germany (estimated at 3.2 million) have criticized the proposed ban.

[9] I would like to thank Dr. iur. Oliver H. Gerstenberg for several very helpful e-mail exchanges on the rationale behind the reasoning of the court.

citizenship rights – the entitlement to the full protection of the law and her cultural identity as an observant Muslim woman – clashed with one another. By leaving it up to the provincial legislatures to decide the extent to which articles of religious clothing and other items could be worn or brought into the schools, the German Constitutional Court underlined the cultural and moral expectations of the parents as well as children involved. The right to freedom of conscience, despite all acknowledgment of the state's neutrality toward religious and other worldviews, was thereby subordinated to the interests of the democratic people in maintaining their specific cultural identities and traditions. The court failed to present a robust constitutional defense of pluralism. This would have involved differentiating more sharply between the status of German citizenship versus the cultural, ethnic, and religious identity of individuals involved. Of course, insofar as in Germany as well as in many other liberal democracies discrimination on the basis of race, gender, ethnicity, and religion is unconstitutional, this formal separation is to some extent encoded in the law. Nevertheless, in the context of being a civil servant of the German state, a thicker and more substantive understanding of citizenship-identity was invoked, and this apparently precluded the teacher's public manifestation of her belonging not just to any religion, but to Islam.[10]

[10] Emcke points out that in an earlier decision concerning the presence of crucifixes in the classroom, what the German Constitutional Court declared to be unconstitutional was not the existence of religious symbols in public spaces or public schools, but rather the *obligation* to display the crucifix regularly. "In this sense," she concludes, "there are no constitutional grounds against religious symbols as such" (Emcke 2000, 284).

The Fereshta Ludin case suggests that the equal claim of citizens to occupy the public office for which they qualify and their specific ethnocultural identities do not simply harmoniously coexist with one another even in liberal democracies. The privileges of membership and ethnocultural identity can and do clash. In the decisions, to be considered below, concerning the right of resident foreigners to vote in municipal and district elections, the German Constitutional Court noted a further clash between the exercise of democratic voice and not being a member of the nation, which, in turn, was characterized as a community of fate and memory.

Who can be a German citizen? Redefining the nation

On October 31, 1990, the German Constitutional Court ruled against a law passed by the provincial assembly of Schleswig-Holstein on February 21, 1989, changing the qualifications for participating in local municipal (*Bezirk*) and district (*Kreis*) elections (BVerfG, 83, 11, Nr. 3, p. 37).[11] According to Schleswig-Holstein's election laws in effect since May 31,

---

[11] A similar change in its election laws was undertaken by the free state of Hamburg so as to enable those of its foreign residents of at least eight years' standing to participate in the election of local municipal assemblies (*Bezirkversammlungen*). Since Hamburg is not a federal province (*Land*) but a free city-state, with its own constitution, some of the technical aspects of this decision are not parallel to those in Schleswig-Holstein. I chose to focus on the latter case alone. It is nonetheless important to note that the federal government, which had opposed Schleswig-Holstein's electoral reforms, supported those of Hamburg. See BVerfG 83, 60, 11, Nr. 4, pp. 60–81.

1985, all those who were defined as German in accordance with article 116 of the Basic Law, who had reached the age of eighteen and who had resided in the electoral district for at least three months, were eligible to vote. The law of February 21, 1989, proposed to amend this as follows: all foreigners residing in Schleswig-Holstein for at least five years, who possessed a valid permit of residency or who were in no need of one, and who were citizens of Denmark, Ireland, the Netherlands, Norway, Sweden, and Switzerland, would be able to vote in local and district elections. The choice of these six states was made on the grounds of reciprocity. Since these countries permit their foreign residents to vote in local and in some cases regional elections, the provincial legislators saw it as appropriate to reciprocate.

The claim that the new election law was anti-constitutional was brought by 224 members of the German parliament, all of them members of the conservative CDU/CSU (Christian Democratic Union/Christian Social Union) party; it was supported by the federal government of Germany. The court justified its decision with the argument that the proposed change of the electoral law contradicted "the principle of democracy," as laid out in articles 20 and 28 of Germany's Basic Law, and according to which "All state power [*Staatsgewalt*] proceeds from the people" (BVerfG 83, 37, Nr. 3, p. 39). Furthermore, "The people [*das Volk*], which the Basic Law of the Federal Republic of Germany recognizes to be the bearer of the authority [*Gewalt*] from which issues the constitution, as well as the people which is the subject of the legitimation and creation of the state, is the German people. Foreigners do not belong to it. Membership in the community of the state [*Staatsverband*] is defined through the right of citizenship . . . Citizenship in the state [*Staatsangehörigkeit*] constitutes a fundamentally indissoluble personal right between the citizen and the state. The vision [image, *Bild*] of the people of the state [*Staatsvolkes*], which underlies this right of belonging to the state, is the political community of fate [*die politische Schicksalsgemeinschaft*], to which individual citizens are bound. Their solidarity with and their embeddedness in [*Verstrickung*] the fate of their home country, which they cannot escape [*sich entrinnen können*], are also the justification for restricting the vote to citizens of the state. They must bear the consequences of their decisions. By contrast, foreigners, regardless of how long they may have resided in the territory of the state, can always return to their homeland" (BVerfG 83, 37, Nr. 3, pp. 39–40).

This resounding statement can be separated into three components: first, a definition of *popular sovereignty* (all power proceeds from the people); second, a *procedural* definition of who is a member of the state; third, a philosophical disquisition on the nature of the bond between the state and the individual, based on the vision of a "political community of fate." The court argued that, according to popular sovereignty, there needs to be a "congruence" between the principle of democracy, the concept of the people, and the main guidelines for voting rights at all levels of state power – namely, federal, provincial, district, and local. Different conceptions of popular sovereignty cannot be employed at different levels of the state. Permitting long-term resident foreigners to vote implies that popular sovereignty would be defined in a different way at the district and local levels than at the provincial and federal levels. In an almost direct repudiation of the Habermasian discursive-democracy principle, the court declares that article 20 of Germany's Basic Law does not imply that "the decisions of state organs must be legitimized through those whose interests are affected [*Betroffenen*] in each case; rather their authority must proceed from the people as a group bound to each other as a unity [*das Volk als eine zur Einheit verbundene Gruppe von Menschen*]" (BVerfG 83, 37, II, Nr. 3, p. 51).

The parliament of the *Land* of Schleswig-Holstein challenges the court's understanding and argues that neither the principle of democracy nor that of the people excludes the rights of foreigners to participate in elections: "The model underlying the Basic Law is the construction of a democracy of human beings, and not that of the collective of the nation. This basic principles does not permit that one distinguish in the long run between the people of the state [*Staatsvolk*] and an association of subservients [*Untertanenverband*]" (BVerfG, 83, 37, II, Nr. 3, p. 42).

The German Constitutional Court eventually resolved this controversy about the meaning of popular sovereignty in favor of a unitary and functionally undifferentiated conception, but it did concede that the sovereign people, through its representatives, could change the definition of citizenship. Procedurally, "the people" simply means all those who have the requisite state membership. If one is a citizen, one has the right to vote; if not, not. "So the Basic Law . . . leaves it up to the legislature to determine more precisely the rules for the acquisition and loss of citizenship and thereby also the criteria of belonging to the people. The law of citizenship is thus the site at which the legislature can do justice to the transformations in the composition of the population of the Federal Republic of Germany." This can be accomplished by expediting the acquisition of citizenship by all those foreigners who are long-term permanent residents of Germany (BVerfG 83, 37, II, Nr. 3, p. 52).

The court here explicitly addresses the paradox of democratic legitimacy, namely that those whose rights to inclusion or exclusion from the *demos* are being decided upon will not themselves be the ones to decide upon these rules. The democratic *demos* can change its self-definition by altering the criteria for admission to citizenship. The court still holds on to the classical model of citizenship according to which democratic-participation rights and nationality are strictly bundled together, but, by signaling the procedural legitimacy of changing the laws governing naturalization of foreigners, the court also acknowledges the power of the democratic sovereign to alter its self-definition so as to accommodate the changing composition of the population. The line separating citizens and foreigners can be renegotiated by the citizens themselves.

Yet this element of democratic openness signaled by the court stands in great contrast to another conception of the democratic people, also adumbrated by the court, which views it as "a political community of fate," that is held together by bonds of solidarity in which individuals are embedded (*Verstricktheit*). Here the democratic people is viewed as an *ethnos*, as a community held together by the power of shared fates, memories, solidarity, and belonging. Such a community is not one that permits free entry and exit. Perhaps marriage with a member of such a community may produce some integration over generations; but, by and large, membership in an *ethnos* – in a community of memory, fate, and belonging – is something one is born into, although as an adult one may renounce this heritage, exit it, or wish to alter it. To what an extent should one view liberal-democratic polities as *ethnoi* communities? Despite its emphatic evocations of the nation as "a community of fate," the court emphasizes that the democratic legislature has the prerogative to transform the meaning of citizenship and the rules of democratic belonging. Such transformations in citizenship may be necessary to do justice to the changed nature of the population. The *demos* and the *ethnos* do not simply overlap.

In retrospect, this decision of the German Constitutional Court, written in 1990, appears as a swan song to a vanishing ideology of nationhood. In 1993 the Treaty of Maastricht, or the Treaty on the European Union, established European citizenship, which granted voting rights and rights to run for office for all members of the fifteen signatory states residing in the territory of other member countries. Of the six countries to whose citizens Schleswig-Holstein wanted to grant reciprocal voting rights – Denmark, Ireland, the Netherlands, Norway, Sweden, and Switzerland – only Norway and Switzerland remained non-beneficiaries of the Maastricht Treaty since they were not EU members.

In the decade following, an intense process of democratic iteration unfolded in the then-unified Germany, during which the challenge posed by the German Constitutional Court to the democratic legislature, of bringing the definition of citizenship in line with the composition of the population, was taken up, rearticulated, and reappropriated. The city-state of Hamburg, in its parallel plea to alter its local election laws, stated this very clearly. "The Federal Republic of Germany has in fact become in the past decades a country of immigration. Those who are affected by the law which is being attacked here are thus not strangers but cohabitants [*Inländer*], who only lack German citizenship. This is especially the case for those foreigners of the second and third generation born in Germany" (BVerfG 83, 60, II, Nr. 4, p. 98). The *demos* is not an *ethnos*, and those living in our midst and who do not belong to the *ethnos* are not strangers either; they are rather "cohabitants," or as later political expressions would have it, "our cocitizens of foreign origin" (*ausländische Mitbürger*). Even these terms, which may sound odd to ears not accustomed to any distinctions besides those of citizens, residents, and non-residents, suggest the transformations of German public consciousness in the 1990s. This intense and soul-searching public debate finally led to an acknowledgment of the *fact* as well as *desirability* of immigration. The need to naturalize second- and third-generation children of immigrants was recognized and the new German citizenship law was passed in January 2000. Ten years after the German Constitutional Court turned down the election law reforms of Schleswig-Holstein and the city-state of Hamburg on the grounds that resident foreigners were not citizens, and thus ineligible to vote, Gemany's membership in the European Union led to the disaggregation of citizenship rights. Resident members of EU states can vote in local as well as EU-wide elections; furthermore, Germany now accepts that it is a country of immigration, that immigrant children are German citizens according to *jus soli*, and that long-term residents who are third-country nationals can naturalize if they wish to do so.

Resignifying rights and identity

In this chapter I have elucidated processes of democratic iteration which attest to a dialectic of rights and identities. In such processes, both the identities involved and the very meaning of rights claims are reappropriated, resignified, and imbued with new and different meanings (see ch. 4). Political agents, caught in such public battles, very often enter the fray with a certain understanding of who they are and what they stand for; but the process itself frequently alters these self-understandings. Thus, in the scarf affair in France, we witness the increasing courage, maybe even militancy, of a group of women considered usually to be "docile subjects," in Michel Foucault's sense (1977, 135–170). Traditional Muslim girls and women are not supposed to appear in the public sphere at all; ironically, precisely the realities of western democracies, with their more liberal and tolerant visions of women's roles, permit these girls and women to be educated in public schools, to enter the labor force, and in the case of Fereshta Ludin in Germany, even to become a German teacher with the status of a civil servant. They are transformed from "docile bodies" into "public selves." Although their struggle at first is to retain their *traditional identities*, whether they choose it or not, as women they also become empowered in ways they may not have anticipated. They learn to *talk back to the state*. My prediction is that it is only a matter of time before the public selves of these women, who are learning to talk back to the state, will also engage and contest the very meaning of the Islamic traditions which they are now fighting to uphold. Eventually, these public battles will initiate private gender struggles about the status of women's rights within the Muslim tradition.[12] These cases also show that outsiders are not at the borders of the polity, but within. In fact the very binarism between nationals and foreigners, citizens and migrants, is sociologically inadequate and the reality is much more fluid, since many citizens are of migrant origin, and many nationals themselves are foreign-born. The practices of immigration and multiculturalism in contemporary democracies flow into one another (see Benhabib 2002a). While the scarf affairs both in France and Germany challenge the vision of a homogeneous people, the German Constitutional Court decisions show that there may often be an incongruity between those who have the formal privilege of democratic citizenship (the *demos*) and others who

---

[12] The French scarf affair is being followed very closely in Turkey, a secular, multiparty democracy, the majority of whose population is Muslim. Throughout the 1980s and 1990s, Turkey confronted its own version of the scarf affair as the Islamist parties increased their power in the parliament and unprecedented numbers of Turkish Islamist women began attending the universities. From the standpoint of Turkish state authorities, the scarf is seen as a violation of the principle of "laiklik" (*laïcité*) articulated by Atatürk, the founder of the republic. The Turkish Constitutional Court decided in 1989 against the use of scarves as well as turbans in universities. Students and the Islamist organizations representing them appealed to article 24 of the Turkish constitution, which guarantees freedom of religious expression, and to article 10, which prohibits discrimination due to religious belief and differences in language, ethnicity, and gender. They were rejected. For further discussion see Benhabib 2002a, 203.

are members of the population but who do not formally belong to the *demos*. In this case, the challenge posed by the German court to the democratic legislature, of adjusting the formal definition of German citizenship so as to reflect the changing realities of the population, was taken up, and the citizenship law was reformed. The democratic people can reconstitute itself through such acts of democratic iteration so as to enable the extension of democratic voice. Aliens can become residents, and residents can become citizens. Democracies require porous borders. This is very well stated by the free city-state of Hamburg, which in a direct challenge to the German Constitutional Court, and in a passage worth repeating, states: "The Federal Republic of Germany has in fact become in the past decades a country of immigration. Those who are affected by the law which is being attacked here are thus not strangers but cohabitants [*Inländer*], who only lack German citizenship. This is especially the case for those foreigners of the second and third generation born in Germany" (BVerfG 83, 60, II, Nr. 4, p. 98).

The constitution of "we, the people," is a far more fluid, contentious, contested, and dynamic process than either Rawlsian liberals or decline-of-citizenship theorists would have us believe. As I argued in chapter 3, the Rawlsian vision of peoples as self-enclosed moral universes is not only empirically but also normatively flawed. This vision cannot do justice to the dual identity of a people as an *ethnos*, as a community of shared fate, memories, and moral sympathies on the one hand, and as the *demos*, as the democratically enfranchised totality of all citizens, who may or may not belong to the same *ethnos*. All liberal democracies that are modern nation-states exhibit these two dimensions. The politics of peoplehood consists in their negotiation. The people is not a self-enclosed and self-sufficient entity. The presence of so many migrants from Algeria, Tunisia, and Morocco, as well as from central Africa, testifies to France's imperial past and conquests, just as the presence of so many *Gastarbeiter* in Germany is a reflection of the economic realities of Germany since World War II. Some would even argue that without their presence, the post-World War II German miracle would not have been conceivable (Hollifield 1992). Peoplehood is dynamic and not a static reality.

Decline-of-citizenship theorists, such as Michael Walzer, are just as wrong as Rawlsian liberals in conflating the *ethnos* and the *demos*. The presence of others who do not share the dominant culture's memories and morals poses a challenge to the democratic legislatures to rearticulate the meaning of democratic universalism. Far from leading to the disintegration of the culture of democracy, such challenges reveal the depth and the breadth of the culture of democracy. Only polities with strong democracies are capable of such universalist rearticulation through which they refashion the meaning of their own peoplehood. Will French political traditions be less strong if they are now carried forth and reappropriated by Algerian women or women from the Côte d'Ivoire? Will German history be less confusing and puzzling if it is taught by an Afghani-German woman? Rather than the decline of citizenship, I see in these instances the reconfiguration of citizenship through democratic iterations.

Conclusion:
cosmopolitan federalism

On April 4, 2003, US newspapers reported the case of Lance
Corporal Jose Gutierrez, aged twenty-seven, who died in a tank
battle outside Umm Qasr in Iraq on March 21, 2003 (Weiner
2003). Corporal Gutierrez was an undocumented immigrant
from Guatemala, an orphan who had reached the United States
through clandestine means and who joined the Marines in
California. His case is by no means unusual: over a dozen
legal and undocumented immigrants – mainly from Mexico
and Central America – who were members of the US armed
forces stationed in Iraq have lost their lives since March 2003.
It is estimated that about 37,000 immigrants serve in the US
armed forces, making up about 3 percent of the population
on active duty (Swarns 2003). Their sad stories led both conservative and liberal lawmakers to propose hastily passed bills
to grant these slain soldiers, and in some cases their spouses
and children, posthumous citizenship. Some suggested that
immigrants who join the armed forces be granted citizenship
immediately, while still others advocated the reduction of the
current waiting period for the granting of citizenship to those
in the military from three to two years.

This is by no means the first time that immigrants
have served in the US army. With the abolition of universal
conscription, however, joining the army has become a venue
of upward mobility for large numbers of low-income legal and
undocumented migrants. We thus have the disturbing case of

individuals dying for a country that denies them voting rights, that is, if they are legal permanent residents waiting to become "naturalized"; and if they are undocumented migrants, as was the case with Corporal Gutierrez, they do not even have the right to obtain a driving license or to open a bank account.

The hasty efforts of American lawmakers to respond to these anomalous and intuitively unfair situations are indicative of the more general scrambling of the lines between territoriality, sovereignty, and citizenship which this book has attempted to clarify. Those who carry out the ultimate sacrifice for the democratic people by giving their lives for it are not always its members in good standing. Furthermore, some are asked to die for a country that denies them the right to vote on those very laws which order them to take up arms against another people. Unlike within the EU, the disaggregation of the institution of citizenship in the United States does not result in voting rights for legal residents – neither at the local nor at state level. Despite being the largest immigrant nation in the world, the American conception of citizenship has remained remarkably unitary at the level of granting political rights, by making "naturalization" a precondition for political voice. This practice is usually defended with the argument that since the granting of citizenship to legal migrants is fairly open, transparent, and speedy in the United States, it is not unfair to make the acquisition of citizenship a precondition for political voice (see the exchange of Motomura 1998 and Tichenor 1998).

This defense, however, does not attend to the facts on the ground: there are at the present an estimated 7 million undocumented immigrants in the United States, many of whom are active and contributing members of the labor force, in farms, hospitals, hotels, and sanitation facilities, others of whom send their children to school, who are active in the community and on school boards. The status of being an undocumented immigrant does not mean having no voice at all. However, these individuals, who may service hospitals whether as nurses or as orderlies, are themselves scared to become sick and dependent on hospital facilities. Not having one's papers in order in our societies is a form of civil death.

The causes of their "illegality" can vary from illogical bureaucratic mishaps and mistakes to their desperate attempts to escape their home countries via smugglers known as "coyotes." The status of illegality does not stamp the other as an alien. Clearly, a democratic adjustment of the practices of legal incorporation is needed so as to normalize undocumented immigrants.

While undocumented-migrant status means civil death and political silencing, the lack of political voice for legal permanent residents means their effective disenfranchisement. An increasing number of individuals wish to retain dual citizenship or to live in one country on a long-term basis while not abdicating their original nationality. Making the exercise of democratic voice dependent upon one's nationality status alone, as the United States laws do, flies in the face of the complex interdependence of the lives of peoples across borders and territories. While the United States has remained impervious to many calls to facilitate dual citizenship, countries such as Mexico and the Dominican Republic permit their large diasporic populations to retain certain citizenship rights at home, including voting in local and national elections and, in the case of the Dominican Republic and Colombia, even running for and holding office. Throughout Southeast Asia, India, and Latin America, "flexible citizenship" (Ong 1999) is emerging as the norm.

These empirical developments are not only indicators of trends toward the disaggregation of citizenship; whether recognized as such by democratic lawmakers or not, they also herald transformations of *democratic sovereignty*. Democratic sovereignty is based on three regulative ideals: that the people are the author as well as the subject of the laws; the ideal of a unified *demos*; and the idea of a self-enclosed and autochthonous territory over which the *demos* governs. I have argued throughout this book that the latter two ideals are indefensible both on normative and on empirical grounds. The unity of the *demos* ought to be understood not as if it were a harmonious given, but rather as a process of self-constitution, through more or less conscious struggles of inclusion and exclusion.

Furthermore, the ideal of territorial self-sufficiency flies in the face of the tremendous interdependence of the peoples of the world – a process which has been speeded up by the phenomenon of globalization. The emergence of international law and the spread of international human rights norms are developments which parallel the spread of globalization. As economic, military, and communicational interdependence increase, as tourism and crossborder mobility are intensified, a body of norms and regulations emerges to govern the activity of international civil society. The traditional view, which traces the legitimacy of international law to treaties among sovereign states alone, is no longer adequate to understand the legal complexities of a global civil society. Along with the obsolescence of this model, the ideal of territorial autochthony must be discarded as well.

The core of democratic self-governance is the ideal of public autonomy, namely, the principle that those who are subject to the law should also be its authors. How can democratic voice and public autonomy be reconfigured if we dispense with the faulty ideals of a people's homogeneity and territorial autochthony? Can democratic representation be organized so as to transcend the nation-state configuration?[1] Throughout this book I have suggested that the new reconfiguration of democratic voice gives rise to subnational as well as transnational modes of citizenship. Within the European Union in particular, there is a return to citizenship in the city and in the transnational institutions of the EU. "Flexible citizenship," particularly in the case of Central American countries, is another such attempt to multiply voice and the sites for the exercise of democratic citizenship.

What all these models have in common, though, is that they retain the principle of territorial membership for

---

[1] The concepts of "divisible sovereignty," "disaggregation of sovereignty," and "unbundling of sovereignty" are now circulating in political and legal theory. Michael Lind makes the argument that the "unbundling of sovereignty" and the delegation by a people of certain attributes of sovereignty, such as self-defense or the right to negotiate with the World Trade Organization, for example, to diverse multi- and supranational instances, as long as such delegation is consensual and revocable, does not destroy the idea of popular sovereignty. But no limits are set on that which cannot be delegated if a people is to remain sovereign. How much law-giving power can indeed be delegated to instances other than those who democratically represent the people before we have forsaken democratic representation altogether? See Lind 2004, 11–14.

undergirding representation. Whether it is residency in cities such as Amsterdam, London, or Frankfurt, or dual citizenship between Mexico, El Salvador, the Dominican Republic, and the USA, the model of democratic representation which I have implicitly assumed is dependent upon access to, residency upon, and eventual membership within a circumscribed territory.

Non-territorially based models of representation are certainly possible: one can be represented by some individual or a body of individuals by virtue of one's linguistic identity, ethnic heritage (as was proposed by Otto Bauer[2] for the nationalities of middle and central Europe after World War I); religious affiliation, professional activities, and affected interests. Representation can run along many lines besides territorial residency. The discourse principle of legitimacy, which enjoins that all those who are affected by the consequences of the adoption of a norm have a say in its articulation (see Introduction), certainly leads to the multiplication of sites of representation and discursive involvement. For example, the community of those affected by the fall of acid rain cuts across the Canadian/USA border and unites these individuals around shared interests, concerns, and activities. Globalization, insofar as it increases both the intensity and the interconnectedness

[2] Otto Bauer (1881–1938) was one of the foremost members of the Austro-Marxist school, which developed in Vienna at the end of the nineteenth century. Others are Max Adler, Rudolf Hilferding, and Karl Renner. Bauer is best known for his study on the problem of nationalities, which was published in 1907 under the title *Die Nationalitätenfrage und die Sozialdemokratie* (The Nationalities Question and Social Democracy).

of human actions around the world, results in the creation of new sites and new logics of representation.

Yet there is a crucial link between democratic self-governance and territorial representation. Precisely because democracies enact laws that are supposed to bind those who legitimately authorize them, the scope of democratic legitimacy cannot extend beyond the *demos* which has circumscribed itself as a people upon a given territory. Democratic laws require closure precisely because democratic representation, must be accountable to a specific people. Imperial legislation, by contrast, was issued from a center and was binding as far as the power of that center to control its periphery extended. Empires have frontiers; democracies have boundaries. I see no way to cut this Gordian knot linking territoriality, representation, and democratic voice. Certainly, representative institutions based on other principles will exist and they ought to proliferate.

In a well-functioning democracy there will be a contentious dialogue, a series of contested iterations, between the *demos* and other representative bodies about the limits of their jurisdiction and authority. While no one instance within the separation of powers can claim ultimate authority for itself, all democracies need to recognize some instances which have the final say. But, as in the case of the German Constitutional Court decisions we considered in the previous chapter, finality does not mean irreversibility or infallibility. The complex dialogue between the democratically elected representatives of the people, the judiciary, and other civil and political actors is a never-ending one of complex and contentious iterations. Within such dialogues, the democratic *demos* can reconstitute itself by enfranchising groups without voice or by providing amnesty for undocumented migrants. But, while the scope of the authority of the laws can be reflexively altered, it is inconceivable that democratic legitimacy can be sustained without some clear demarcation of those in the name of whom the laws have been enacted from those upon whom the laws are not binding.

Why did Kant claim that a world government would be a "universal monarchy" and a "soulless despotism"? Montesquieu's model of political rule may have played a role here ([1748] 1965, I, 19–28; II, 10–11). Montesquieu argued that empires were compatible with vast territories, while republics required countries of moderate size. In empires, only one was free and the rest obeyed; in republics all would be free. The more extensive the territory, the more frayed interconnections among individuals would become, and the more indifferent they would grow to each other's lot. In contemporary language, we may say that interest in democratic voice as well as solidarity with others would disappear.

The intuition that there may be a crucial link between territorial size and form of government is old in the history of western political thought, and it is one that I accept. Unlike communitarians and liberal nationalists, however, who view this link primarily as being based upon a cultural bond of identity, I am concerned with the logic of democratic representation, which requires closure for the sake of maintaining democratic legitimacy. Certainly, identification and solidarity are not unimportant, but they need to be leavened through democratic attachments and constitutional norms. In the spirit of Kant, therefore, I have pleaded for moral universalism and cosmopolitan federalism. I have not advocated *open* but rather *porous* borders; I have pleaded for first-admittance rights for refugees and asylum seekers but have accepted the right of democracies to regulate the transition from first admission to full membership; I have also argued for subjecting laws governing naturalization to human rights norms and rejected the claim of a sovereign people not to permit naturalization and to bar the eventual citizenship of aliens in its midst. For some, these proposals will go too far in the direction of rootless cosmopolitanism; for others, they will not go far enough. I believe that the best way to approach political membership at the dawn of a new century is by accepting the challenge of conflicting moral visions and political commitments suggested by one of the slogans of the Immigrant Workers' Freedom Ride: "No human is illegal" (New York, October 4, 2003). This book has attempted to reconcile the vision inspiring this principle with the institutional and normative necessities of democracy, as a form of government based upon public autonomy, namely that those subject to the laws also be their authors.

BIBLIOGRAPHY

Al-Hibri, Azizah Y. 1999. "Is Western Patriarchal Feminism Good for Third World/Minority Women?" In: Okin, et al. 1999: 41–46.

Aleinikoff, Alexander T. 2002. *Semblances of Sovereignty: The Constitution, the State, and American Citizenship.* Harvard University Press. Cambridge, MA.

Arendt, Hannah. [1945] 1978. "Zionism Reconsidered." In: *The Jew as Pariah: Jewish Identity and Politics in the Modern Age.* Ed. by Ron H. Feldman. Grove Press. New York: 131–192.

[1951] 1968. *The Origins of Totalitarianism.* Harcourt, Brace and Jovanovich. New York.

1961. "Crisis in Culture." In: *Between Past and Future: Six Exercises in Political Thought.* Meridian Books. New York.

1994. "Nightmare and Flight." In: *Hannah Arendt: Essays in Understanding, 1930–1954.* Ed. by Jerome Kohn. Harcourt, Brace and Jovanovich. New York: 133–136.

Aristotle. 1941. *Politics.* Trans. by Benjamin Jowett. In: *Basic Works of Aristotle.* Ed. by Richard McKeon. Random House. New York: 1127–1325.

Bader, Veit. 1995. "Citizenship and Exclusion. Radical Democracy, Community and Justice: Or, What Is Wrong with Communitarianism?" *Political Theory.* 23(2): 211–246.

1997. "Fairly Open Borders." In: *Citizenship and Exclusion.* Ed. by V. M. Bader. Macmillan. London: 28–62.

Forthcoming. "The More Inclusion, the Less Motivation? A Big Trade-Off? Liberal Nationalism and Transnational Institutions and Obligations." In: *Identities, Allegiances and Affiliations.*

Ed. by Seyla Benhabib and Ian Shapiro. Cambridge University Press. Cambridge, UK.

Balibar, Etienne. 1996. "Is European Citizenship Possible?" *Public Culture.* 8: 355–376.

Barber, Benjamin. 1995. *Jihad vs. McWorld.* Times Books. New York.

Bauboeck, Rainer. 1994. *Transnational Citizenship: Membership and Rights in International Migration.* Edward Elgar. Aldershot, UK.

1998. "The Crossing and Blurring of Boundaries in International Migration: Challenges for Social and Political Theory." In: *Blurred Boundaries: Migration, Ethnicity, Citizenship.* Ed. by Rainer Bauboeck and John Rundell. Ashgate Publications. Vienna: 17–52.

Beitz, Charles. [1979] 1999. *Political Theory and International Relations.* Revised edn. Princeton University Press. Princeton, NJ.

2000. "Rawls's Law of Peoples." *Ethics.* 110(4) (July): 669–696.

Benhabib, Seyla. 1984. "Obligation, Contract and Exchange, The Opening Arguments of Hegel's *Philosophy of Right.*" In: *Civil Society and the State. Hegel's Political Philosophy.* Ed. by Z. A. Pelczynski. Cambridge University Press. Cambridge, UK: 159–177.

1992. *Situating the Self: Gender, Community and Postmodernism in Contemporary Ethics.* Routledge and Polity. New York and London.

1995. "Cultural Complexity, Moral Interdependence, and the Global Dialogical Community." In: *Women, Culture and Development: A Study of Human Capabilities.* Ed. by Martha Nussbaum and Jonathan Glover. Clarendon Press. Oxford, UK, 235–259.

[1996] 2003. *The Reluctant Modernism of Hannah Arendt.* Sage Publications. Thousand Oaks, CA. New edition by Rowman and Littlefield.

1999a. "Germany Opens Up." *The Nation.* June 21: 6.

1999b. *Kulturelle Vielfalt und demokratische Gleichheit: Die Horkheimer Vorlesungen.* Fischer. Frankfurt am Main.

1999c. "The Liberal Imagination and the Four Dogmas of Multiculturalism." *Yale Journal of Criticism.* 12(2): 401–413.

1999d. "'Nous' et 'les Autres': The Politics of Complex Cultural Dialogue in a Global Civilization." In: *Multicultural Questions.* Ed. by Christian Joppke and Steven Lukes. Oxford University Press. Oxford, UK: 44–62.

1999e. "Sexual Difference and Collective Identities: The New Global Constellation." *Signs: Journal of Women in Culture and Society.* 24(2): 335–361.

2001a. "Dismantling the Leviathan: Citizen and State in a Global World." *Responsive Community.* 11(3): 14–27.

2001b. "Ungrounded Fears. American Intellectuals and the Spectre of European Harmonization: A Response to Michael Walzer and Noah M. Pickus." *Responsive Community.* 11(4): 85–91.

2002a. *The Claims of Culture: Equality and Diversity in the Global Era.* Princeton University Press. Princeton, NJ.

2002b. "Transformations of Citizenship: The Case of Contemporary Europe." *Government and Opposition.* 37(4)(Fall): 439–465.

2003. "In Search of Europe's Borders. The Politics of Migration in the European Union." *Dissent.* Fall. 33–39.

2004. "The *Law of Peoples*, Distributive Justice and Migrations." In: *Fordham Law Review.* Symposium on Rawls and the Law. *Fordham Law Review.* 72(5)(April). 1761–1788.

Bentham, Jeremy. 1843. *The Works of Jeremy Bentham.* Ed. by John Bowring, 11 vols. W. Tait. Edinburgh and London. Vol. II.

Bohman, James and Lutz-Bachmann, Matthias, eds. 1997. *Perpetual Peace: Essays on Kant's Cosmopolitan Ideal.* MIT Press. Cambridge, MA.

Brubaker, Rogers. 1992. *Citizenship and Nationhood in France and Germany.* Harvard University Press. Cambridge, MA.

Brun-Rovet, Marianne. 2000. "A Perspective on the Multiculturalism Debate: *L'affaire da foulard* and *laïcité* in France, 1989–1999." Seminar paper. Harvard University, Department of Government. On file with the author.

Buchanan, Allan. 2000. "Rawls's Law of Peoples: Rules for a Vanished Westphalian World." *Ethics*. 110 (July): 697–721.

———. 2001. "From Nuremberg to Kosovo: The Morality of Illegal International Reform." *Ethics*. 111 (July): 673–705.

Carens, Joe. 1995. "Aliens and Citizens: The Case for Open Borders." In: *Theorizing Citizenship*. Ed. by Ronald Beiner. SUNY Press. Albany, NY: 229–255.

Cesarani, David and Fulbrook, Mary. 1996. *Citizenship, Nationality and Migration in Europe*. Routledge. London and New York.

Cole, Philip. 2000. *Philosophies of Exclusion: Liberal Political Theory and Immigration*. Edinburgh University Press. Edinburgh.

Coleman, Doriane Lambelet. 1996. "Individualizing Justice Through Multiculturalism: The Liberals' Dilemma." *Columbia Law Review*. 96(5) (June 1996): 1093–1167.

Cover, Robert M. 1983. "*Nomos* and Narrative." *Harvard Law Review*. 97(1): 4–68.

De Beauvoir, Simone. 1949. *Le Deuxième Sexe*. Editions Gallimard. Paris.

de Jong, Cornelius. 2000. "Harmonization of Asylum and Immigration Policies: The Long and Winding Road from Amsterdam via Vienna to Tampere." In: *The Asylum Acquis Handbook*. Ed. by Peter J. van Krieken. T. M. C. Asser Press. The Hague: 21–37.

Derrida, Jacques. [1982] 1991. "Signature, Event, Context." In: *A Derrida Reader: Between the Blinds*. Ed. and intro. by Peggy Kamuf. Columbia University Press. New York: 80–111.

"Derrière la voile." 2001. *Le Monde Diplomatique*. 599(51)(February): 6–10.

225

Doyle, Michael. 2001. "The New Interventionism." In: *Global Justice.* Ed. by Thomas W. Pogge. Basil Blackwell. Oxford, UK, and Cambridge, MA: 219–242.

Drèze, Jean and Sen, Amartya. 1989. *Hunger and Public Action.* Oxford University Press. New York.

Dworkin, Ronald. 2002. "The Threat to Patriotism." *New York Times Review of Books.* February 28.

Emcke, Carolin. 2000. *Kollektive Identitäten: Sozialphilosophische Grundlagen.* Campus Verlag. Frankfurt am Main and New York.

Fink, Carole. 1972. "Defender of Minorities: Germany in the League of Nations, 1926–1933." *Central European History.* 5(4): 330–357.

Fiss, Owen. 1998. "The Immigrant as Pariah." *Boston Review.* 23(5)(October/November): 4–6.

——— 1999. *A Community of Equals: The Constitutional Protection of New Americans.* Ed. by Joshua Cohen and Joel Rogers. Beacon Press. Boston: 3–25.

Flikschuh, Katrin. 2000. *Kant and Modern Political Philosophy.* Cambridge University Press. Cambridge, UK.

Forst, Rainer. 1999. "The Basic Right to Justification: Toward a Constructivist Conception of Human Rights." *Constellations.* 6: 35–60.

Foucault, Michel. 1977. *Discipline and Punish: The Birth of the Prison.* Trans. by Alan Sheridan. Pantheon Books. New York.

Friedrichs, Jörg. 2001. "The Meaning of New Medievalism." *European Journal of International Relations.* 7(4)(December): 475–503.

Galston, William. 1991. *Liberal Purposes: Goods, Virtues, and Duties in the Liberal State.* Cambridge University Press. Cambridge, UK.

Gaspard, Françoise and Khosrokhavar, Farhad. 1995. *Le Foulard et la République.* La Découverte. Paris.

Genovese, Eugene. [1965] 1990. *The Political Economy of Slavery: Studies in the Economy and Society of the Slave South.* Pantheon Books. New York.

Genovese-Fox, Elizabeth and Genovese, Eugene D. 1983. *Fruits of Merchant Capital: Slavery and Bourgeois Property in the Rise and Expansion of Capitalism.* Oxford University Press. New York.

Giraud, Veronique and Sintomer, Yves. 2004. *Alma et Lila Levy: Des Filles Comme les Autres.* La Découverte. Paris.

Göle, Nilüfer. 1996. *The Forbidden Modern: Civilization and Veiling.* University of Michigan Press. Ann Arbor.

Guéhenno, Jean-Marie. 1995. *The End of the Nation-State.* Trans. by Victoria Elliott. University of Minnesota Press. Minneapolis.

Guild, Elspeth. 1996. "The Legal Framework of Citizenship of the European Union." In: Cesarani and Fulbrook 1996: 30– 57.

Habermas, Jürgen. [1983] 1990. *Moral Consciousness and Communicative Action.* Trans. by Christian Lenhardt and Shierry Weber Nicholsen. MIT Press. Cambridge, MA.

1996. *Between Facts and Norms: Contributions to a Discourse Theory of Law and Democracy.* Trans. by William Rehg. MIT Press. Cambridge, MA.

1998. "The European Nation-State: On the Past and Future of Sovereignty and Citizenship." In: *The Inclusion of the Other: Studies in Political Theory.* Ed. by Ciaran Cronin and Pablo De Greiff. MIT Press. Cambridge, MA: 105–129.

Hathaway, James. 1991. *The Law of Refugee Status.* Butterworths. Toronto and Vancouver.

1997. *Reconceiving International Refugee Law.* Nijhoff Law Specials, vol. 30. Martinus Nijhoff Publishers. The Hague, Boston and London.

Hegel, G. W. F. [1821] 1973. *Hegel's Philosophy of Right.* Trans. and with notes by T. M. Knox. Oxford University Press. Oxford, UK.

Held, David. 2002. "Law of States, Law of Peoples." *Legal Theory.* 8: 1–44.

Held, David, McGrew, Anthony, Goldblatt, David, and Perraton, Jonathan. 1999. *Global Transformations*. Stanford University Press. Stanford, CA.

Hobbes, Thomas. [1651] 1996. *Leviathan.* Cambridge University Press. Cambridge, UK.

Hobsbawm, Eric. 1975. *The Age of Capital 1848–1875*. Scribner. New York.

———. 1987. *The Age of Empire 1875–1914*. Pantheon Books. New York.

———. 1990. *Nations and Nationalism Since 1780: Programme, Myth, Reality*. Cambridge University Press. Cambridge, UK, and New York.

———. 1996. "The Future of the State." *Development and Change*. 27(2)(April): 267–278.

Hollifield, James F. 1992. *Immigrants, Markets, and States: The Political Economy of Postwar Europe*. Harvard University Press. Cambridge, MA, and London.

Honig, Bonnie. 1999. "My Culture Made Me Do It." In: Okin, et al. 1999: 35–40.

———. 2001. *Democracy and the Foreigner*. Princeton University Press. Princeton, NJ.

Hont, Istvan. 1995. "The Permanent Crisis of a Divided Mankind: 'Contemporary Crisis of the Nation-State' in Historical Perspective." In: *Contemporary Crisis of the Nation-State?* Ed. by John Dunn. Blackwell. Oxford, UK: 166–231.

Jacobson, David. 1997. *Rights Across Borders: Immigration and the Decline of Citizenship*. Johns Hopkins University Press. Baltimore and London.

Jefferson, Thomas. [1774] 1984. "Summary View of the Rights of British America." In *Jefferson: Writings*. Ed. by Merrill D. Peterson. Literary Classics of the United States. New York: 105–122.

Jones-Correa, Michael. 1998. "Why Immigrants Want Dual Citizenship (And We Should Too): A Response to Peter Schuck." In: Pickus 1998: 193–199.

Kakar, Sudhir. 1990. *Intimate Relations: Exploring Indian Sexuality.* University of Chicago Press. Chicago.

Kant, Immanuel. [1795] 1923. "Zum Ewigen Frieden: Ein philosophischer Entwurf." In: *Immanuel Kants Werke.* Ed. by A. Buchenau, E. Cassirer, and B. Kellermann. Verlag Bruno Cassirer. Berlin: 425–474.

[1795] 1957. "Perpetual Peace." Trans. by Lewis White Beck. In: *On History.* Ed. by Lewis White Beck. Library of Liberal Arts. Indianapolis and New York: 85–137.

[1795] 1994. "Perpetual Peace: A Philosophical Sketch." Trans. by H. B. Nisbet. In: *Kant: Political Writings.* Ed. by Hans Reiss. Second and enlarged edn. Cambridge, UK: 93–130.

[1797] 1922. "Die Metaphysik der Sitten in zwei Teilen." In: *Immanuel Kants Werke.* Ed. by A. Buchenau, E. Cassirer, and B. Kellermann. Verlag Bruno Cassirer. Berlin: 5–309.

Kant, Immanuel. [1797] 1994. "Introduction to the Theory of Right" and "The Theory of Right, Part II: Public Right" from "The Metaphysics of Morals." In: *Kant: Political Writings.* Ed. by Hans Reiss. Cambridge University Press. Cambridge, UK: 131–176.

[1797] 1996. *The Metaphysics of Morals.* Trans. and ed. by Mary Gregor. Cambridge University Press. Cambridge, UK.

1949. *Critique of Practical Reason and Other Writings in Moral Philosophy.* Trans. and ed. by Lewis White Beck. University of Chicago Press. Chicago.

Kastoryano, Riva. 2002. *Negotiating Identities.* Princeton University Press. Princeton, NJ.

Kerber, Linda. 1997. *Women of the Republic: Intellect and Ideology in Revolutionary America.* University of North Carolina Press. Chapel Hill, NC.

Kleingeld, Pauline. 1998. "Kant's Cosmopolitan Law: World Citizenship for a Global Legal Order." *Kantian Review.* 2: 72–90.

Krasner, Stephen. 1999. *Sovereignty: Organized Hypocrisy.* Princeton University Press. Princeton, NJ.

Kuper, Andrew. 2000. "Rawlsian Global Justice: Beyond *The Law of Peoples* to a Cosmopolitan Law of Persons." *Political Theory.* 28: 640–674.

Landes, David. 1998. *The Wealth and Poverty of Nations: Why Some Are So Rich and Some Are So Poor.* W. W. Norton. New York.

Landes, Joan. 1988. *Women and the Public Sphere in the Age of the French Revolution.* Cornell University Press. Ithaca, NY.

Lehning, Percy B. and Weale, Albert, eds. 1997. *Citizenship, Democracy and Justice in the New Europe.* Routledge. London.

Lévi-Strauss, Claude. 1969. *Elementary Structures of Kinship.* Beacon Press. Boston.

Lind, Michael. 2004, "Popular Sovereignty, Divisible Sovereignty and the Future of World Order." Paper delivered at the Legal Theory Workshop, Yale Law School, May 6. On file with the author.

Linklater, Andrew. 1998. *The Transformation of Political Community: Ethical Foundations of the Post-Westphalian Era.* Polity Press. Cambridge, UK.

Locke, John. [1690] 1980. *The Second Treatise of Civil Government.* Ed. and with an introduction by C. B. McPherson. Hackett Publishing. Indianapolis and Cambridge, MA.

Macedo, Steve. 1999. *Deliberative Politics: Essays on Democracy and Disagreement.* Oxford University Press. Oxford, UK.

——— 2004. "What Self-Governing Peoples Owe to One Another: Universalism, Diversity, and *The Law of Peoples.*" Symposium on Rawls and the Law. *Fordham Law Review.* 72(5)(April). 1721–1738.

Mann, Michael. 1986. *The Sources of Social Power,* 2 Vols. Cambridge University Press. Cambridge, UK.

Marshall, T. H. 1950. *Citizenship and Social Class and Other Essays.* Cambridge University Press. London.

Martens, Thomas. 1996. "Cosmopolitanism and Citizenship: Kant Against Habermas." *European Journal of Philosophy*. 4(3): 328–347.

Marx, Karl. [1857–1858] 1973. *Grundrisse: Foundations of the Critique of Political Economy*. Penguin Books. Harmondsworth, UK.

Meuschel, Sigrid. 1981. *Kapitalismus oder Sklaverei: Die Langwierige Durchsetzung der Bürgerlichen Gesellschaft in den USA*. Europäische Verlagsanstalt. Frankfurt am Main.

Michelman, Frank. 1988. "Law's Republic." *Yale Law Journal*. 97(8)(July): 1493–1537.

    1996. "Parsing 'A Right to Have Rights.'" *Constellations*. 3(2) (October): 200–209.

Montesquieu, Baron de. [1748] 1965. *The Spirit of the Laws*. Trans. by Thomas Nugent. Intro. by Franz Neuman. 2 vols. in 1. New York. Hafner.

Motomura, Hiroshi. 1998. "Alienage Classification in a Nation of Immigrants: Three Models of 'Permanent Residence.'" In: Pickus 1998: 199–223.

Münz, Rainer. 2001. "Ethnos or Demos? Migration and Citizenship in Germany." Lecture delivered at the Center for European Studies, Harvard University, Cambridge, MA. On file with the author.

Muthu, Sankar. 1999. "Enlightenment and Anti-Imperialism." *Social Research*. 66(4)(Winter): 959–1007.

    2000. "Justice and Foreigners: Kant's Cosmopolitan Right." *Constellations*. 7(1)(March): 23–45.

    2003. *Enlightenment and Empire*. Princeton University Press. Princeton, NJ.

Nagel, Thomas. 1991. *Equality and Partiality*. Oxford University Press. New York.

Neuman, Gerald L. 1993. "Buffer Zones Against Refugees: Dublin, Schengen, and the Germany Asylum Amendment." *Virginia Journal of International Law*. 3: 503–526.

1996. *Strangers to the Constitution: Immigrants, Borders, and Fundamental Law*. Princeton University Press. Princeton, NJ.

2003. "Human Rights and Constitutional Rights: Harmony and Dissonance." *Stanford Law Review*. 55(5)(May): 1863–1901.

Nussbaum, Martha. 1990. "Aristotelian Social Democracy." In: *Liberalism and the Good*. Ed. by R. B. Douglass, G. Mara, and H. Richardson. Routledge. New York: 203–252.

1996. "Patriotism and Cosmopolitanism." In: *For Love of Country: Debating the Limits of Patriotism*. Ed. by Joshua Cohen. Beacon Press. Boston, MA: 3–17.

1997. "Kant and Cosmopolitanism." In: Bohman and Lutz-Bachmann: 25–59.

Offe, Claus. 1998. "Demokratie und Wohlfahrtstaat." In: Streeck: 99–137.

Okin, Susan Moller. 1999. "Is Multiculturalism Bad for Women?" In Okin, et al. 1999: 7–25.

Okin, Susan Moller, Cohen, Joshua, Howard, Matthew and Nussbaum, Martha. 1999. *Is Multiculturalism Bad for Women?* Princeton University Press. Princeton, NJ.

O'Neill, Onora. 1996. *Towards Justice and Virtue: A Constructive Account of Practical Reasoning*. Cambridge University Press. Cambridge, UK.

2000. *Bounds of Justice*. Cambridge University Press. Cambridge, UK.

Ong, Aihwa. 1999. *Flexible Citizenship: The Cultural Logic of Transnationality*. Duke University Press. Durham, NC.

Ortner, Sherry B. 1974. "Is Female to Male as Nature Is to Culture?" In: *Women, Culture, and Society*. Ed. by M. Z. Rosaldo and L. Lamphere. Stanford University Press. Stanford, CA: 67–89.

Palmer, Stephanie. 2002. "Feminism and the Promise of Human Rights: Possibilities and Paradoxes." In: *Visible Women: Essays on Feminist Legal Theory and Political Philosophy*. Ed. by Susan

James and Stephanie Palmer. Hart Publishing. Oxford, UK: 91–117.

Parekh, Bhikhu. 2000. *Rethinking Multiculturalism: Cultural Diversity and Political Theory.* Harvard University Press. Cambridge, MA.

Pensky, Max. 2002. "Constitutional Exclusion? EU Constitution, Human Rights, and the Problem of Scope." Paper delivered at the European Constitutionalism Conference, Johann-Wolfgang Goethe University, Frankfurt am Main, June 11–13. On file with the author.

Perea, Juan F. 1998. "'Am I an American or Not?' Reflections on Citizenship, Americanization and Race." In: Pickus 1998: 49–77.

Pickus, Noah M. J., ed. 1998. *Immigration and Citizenship in the Twenty-First Century.* Rowman and Littlefield. New York and Oxford, UK.

Pogge, Thomas. 1989. *Realizing Rawls.* Cornell University Press. Ithaca, NY.

1992. "Cosmopolitanism and Sovereignty." *Ethics.* 103(October): 48–75.

ed. 2001. *Global Justice.* Blackwell Publishers. Oxford and Cambridge, MA.

2002. "Moral Universalism and Global Economic Justice." *Politics, Philosophy and Ecocnomics.* 1: 29–58.

Post, Robert. 2000. "Between Philosophy and Law: Sovereignty and the Design of Democratic Institutions." In: *Designing Democratic Institutions.* Ed. by Ian Shapiro and Stephen Macedo. New York University Press. New York and London: 209–223.

Preuss, Ulrich. 1995. "Problems of a Concept of European Citizenship." *European Law Journal.* 1(3): 267–281.

Putnam, Robert. 2001. *Bowling Alone: The Collapse and Revival of American Community.* Simon and Schuster. New York.

2003. *Better Together: Restoring the American Community.* Simon and Schuster. New York.

233

Ratner, Steven R. and Abrams, Jason S. [1997] 2002. *Accountability for Human Rights Atrocities in International Law: Beyond the Nuremberg Legacy*. Oxford University Press. Oxford, UK.

Rawls, John [1971] 1972. *A Theory of Justice*. Harvard University Press. Cambridge, MA.

1993. *Political Liberalism*. Columbia University Press. New York.

1999. *The Law of Peoples*. Harvard University Press. Cambridge, MA.

Rieff, David. 2003. "Displaced Places." *New York Times Sunday Magazine*. September 21. Section 6, 36–41.

Rosenau, James. 1997. *Along the Domestic–Foreign Frontier. Exploring Governance in a Turbulent World*. Cambridge University Press. Cambridge, UK.

Sandel, Michael. 1996. *Democracy's Discontent: America in Search of a Public Philosophy*. Belknap Press at Harvard University. Cambridge, MA.

Schabas, William A. 2001. *An Introduction to the International Criminal Court*. Cambridge University Press. Cambridge, UK.

Schama, Simon. 1987. *The Embarrassment of Riches: An Interpretation of Dutch Culture in the Golden Age*. Alfred A. Knopf. New York.

Schmitt, Carl. [1923] 1985. *The Crisis of Parliamentary Democracy*. Trans. by Ellen Kennedy. MIT Press. Cambridge, MA.

[1927] 1996. *The Concept of the Political*. Trans., intro., and notes by George Schwab. University of Chicago Press. Chicago.

Schuck, Peter. 1998. *Citizens, Strangers, and In-Betweens: Essays on Immigration and Citizenship*. Westview Press. Boulder, CO.

Sciolino, Elaine. 2003a. "French Islam Wins Officially Recognized Voice." *New York Times*. April 14. A4.

2003b. "Paris Journal. Back to Barricades: Liberty, Equality, Sisterhood." *New York Times*. August 1. A4.

Scott, Joan. 1988. *Gender and the Politics of History*. Columbia University Press. New York.

Sen, Amartya. 1981. *Poverty and Famine: An Essay on Entitlement and Deprivation.* Oxford University Press. New York.

———. 1984. *Resources, Values and Development.* Harvard University Press. Cambridge, MA.

———. 1999. *Development as Freedom.* Oxford University Press. Oxford, UK.

Shapiro, Ian. 1999. *Democratic Justice.* Yale University Press. New Haven, CT.

Sheffler, Samuel. 2001. *Boundaries and Allegiances: Problems of Justice and Responsibility in Liberal Thought.* Oxford University Press. Oxford, UK.

Sidgwick, Henry. [1874] 1962. *The Methods of Ethics.* University of Chicago Press. Chicago and Toronto.

Smith, Rogers. 2003. *Stories of Peoplehood.* Cambridge University Press. Cambridge, UK.

SOPEMI Publications. 1998 and 2000. The OECD Continuous Reporting System for Migration. *Trends in International Migration. Annual Report.* Organization for Economic Co-operation and Development. Paris.

Soysal, Yasemin. 1994. *Limits of Citizenship: Migrants and Postnational Membership in Europe.* University of Chicago Press. Chicago.

Streeck, Wolfgang, ed. 1998. *Internationale Wirtschaft, nationale Demokratie?* Campus Verlag. Frankfurt am Main.

Swarns, Rachel. 2003. "Aftereffects. Immigration: Allowing Those Who Fight for Their Country to Be a Part of It." *New York Times.* May 7, A20.

Thaa, Winfried. 2001. "'Lean Citizenship': The Fading Away of the Political in Transnational Democracy." *European Journal of International Relations.* 7(4): 503–525.

Tichenor, Daniel. 1998. "Membership and American Social Contracts: A Response to Hiroshi Motomura." In: Pickus 1998: 223–229.

Tillie, Jean and Slijper, Boris. Forthcoming. "Immigrant Political Integration and Ethnic Civic Communities in Amsterdam." In: *Identities, Allegiances and Affliliations.* Ed. by Seyla Benhabib and Ian Shapiro. Cambridge University Press. Cambridge, UK.

Tilly, Charles. 1990. *Coercion, Capital and European States, AD 990–1990.* Blackwell. Cambridge, UK.

———. 1992. "Future European States." *Social Research.* 59: 705–717.

Tuck, Richard. 1979. *Natural Rights Theories.* Cambridge University Press. Cambridge, UK.

Tully, James. 1993. *Approach to Political Philosophy: Locke in Contexts.* Cambridge University Press. Cambridge, UK.

United Nations. 1945. *Charter of International Military Tribunal, in Agreement for the Prosecution and Punishment of the Major War Criminals of the European Axis.* 59 STAT. 1544, 82 UNTS 279.

———. 1948. *International Bill of Human Rights* (also *Universal Declaration of Human Rights*). UN Doc.A/Res/217(iii).

———. 1949. *Geneva Convention for the Amelioration of the Condition of the Wounded and Sick in Armed Forces in the Field.* 6 UST 3114, 75 UNTS 31.

———. 1951. *Convention Relating to the Status of Refugees.* UN Doc.A/Res/429.

———. 1993. *Statute of the International Criminal Tribunal for the Former Yugoslavia.* UN Doc.S/RES/827.

———. 1994. *Statute of the International Criminal Tribunal for Rwanda.* UN Doc.S/RES/955.

United Nations. 1998. *Rome Statute of the International Criminal Court.* 1998. UN Doc.A/CONF.183/9.

United Nations, Department of Economic and Social Affairs. 2002. *International Migration Report.* ST/ESA/SER.A/220.

van Krieken, Peter, ed. 2000. *The Asylum Acquis Handbook: The Foundations for a Common European Asylum Policy.* Asser Press. The Hague.

Waldron, Jeremy. 2001. "Actions and Accommodations." The Kadish Lecture. University of California, Berkeley. February 23. On file with the author.

Walzer, Michael. 1983. *Spheres of Justice: A Defense of Pluralism and Equality.* Basic Books. New York.

———. 1984. "Liberalism and the Art of Separation." *Political Theory.* 12(August): 315–330.

———. 1987. *Interpretation and Social Criticism.* Harvard University Press. Cambridge, MA.

———. 2001. "In Response: Support for Modesty and the Nation-State." *Responsive Community.* 11, 2 (Spring): 28–31.

Weber, Max. [1922] 1958. *From Max Weber: Essays in Sociology.* Trans., ed., and with an introduction by H. H. Gerth and C. Wright Mills. Oxford University Press. Oxford, UK.

———. [1930] 1992. *The Protestant Ethic and the Spirit of Capitalism.* Trans. by Talcott Parsons. Routledge. New York.

———. [1956] 1978. *Economy and Society: An Outline of Interpretive Sociology.* Ed. by Günther Roth and Claus Wittich. [*Wirtschaft und Gesellschaft: Grundriss der verstehenden Soziologie.*] University of California Press. Berkeley.

Weiler, Joseph. 1999. *The Constitution of Europe: Do the New Clothes Have an Emperor? And Other Essays on European Integration.* Cambridge University Press. Cambridge, UK.

Weiner, Tim. 2003. "A Nation at War. Immigrant Marines: Latinos Gave Their Lives to New Land." *New York Times.* April 4. B10.

Wiebe, Robert H. 2002. *Who We Are: A History of Popular Nationalism.* Princeton University Press. Princeton, NJ, and Oxford.

Wischke, Mirko. 2002. "Die Politik der Menschenrechte im Zeitalter der Globalisierung: Zur aktuellen Diskussion in der Politischen Philosophie und Rechtsphilosophie." *Philosophische Rundschau.* 49: 224–244.

Wittgenstein, Ludwig. 1953. *Philosophical Investigations*. Trans. by G. E. M. Anscombe. Blackwell. Oxford, UK.

Wolfe, Alan. 2001. "Alien Nation." *New Republic*. March 26.

Zlotnik, Hania. 2001. "Past Trends in International Migration and Their Implications for Future Prospects." In: *International Migration into the Twenty-First Century: Essays in Honor of Reginald Appleyard*. Edited by M. A. B. Siddique. Edward Elgar. Boston, MA: 227–262.

Zolberg, Aristide R. and Long Litt-Woon. 1999. "Why Islam Is Like Spanish: Cultural Incorporation in Europe and the United States." *Politics and Society*. 27(1) (March): 5–38.

Zolberg, Aristide R. and Benda, Peter M. 2001. *Global Migrants, Global Refugees: Problems and Solutions*. Berghahn Books. New York and Oxford, UK.

Habermas, Jürgen 13, 17, 18, 44
Haiti 119
Hamburg 24, 208–209, 211
Hathaway, James 68
Hegel, G. W. F. 130, 143
Held, David 40
Herzl, Theodor 62
Hitler, Adolf 54
Hobbes, Thomas 129, 130
Hobsbawm, Eric 115
Hollifield, James F. 212
Holocaust 62
homogeneity, national 53, 80, 81,
94, 172, 210, 217
Honig, Bonnie 116
hospitality 21, 25–39, 59, 71, 129, 177
human rights 47, 50, 60, 92, 129–134
and autonomy 133
and citizens' rights 22, 50, 142,
167
and civil rights 168
and colonialism 52
communicative 134, 136
declarations 2, 7
and European integration 150,
167
grounding of 92
and immigration 122
international norms 6, 12, 115,
125, 216, 221
international regime 7–12, 124,
173
to membership 134–143
and nationalism 62
principles 2, 123, 175, 178
right to asylum 69
and right to have rights 55

and sovereignty 41, 42, 47, 61,
65–69, 118, 123
universal 18, 21, 44, 118, 146, 178
humanitarian inverventions 9–10,
42

idealization 77, 82, 84, 91
identity 82, 187, 188
civic 148
collective 65, 82, 145, 173, 174
cultural 62, 124, 126, 166, 193, 201,
220
democratic 126
ethnic 62, 201
in European Union 163–167
French 190
national 174, 190
political 169, 174
religious 201
and rights 167–169, 209
traditional 209
Immigrant Workers' Freedom
Ride 221
immigrants 184
absorption of 136
in European Union 166
incorporation of 136, 156
legal conditions for 150
rights of 56
immigrants, undocumented 152,
154, 213, 214, 215, 220
conditions for 154
immigration 11, 68, 72, 90, 92, 124,
210
conditions for 118, 137
first entry 11, 136, 154
grounds for limiting 88, 89–90

Lightning Source UK Ltd.
Milton Keynes UK
UKOW06f1146281215

265400UK00007B/230/P